D0162124

BURN–OUT

BURN–OUT

Stages of Disillusionment in the Helping Professions

by Jerry Edelwich, M.S.W.
with Archie Brodsky

 **HUMAN SCIENCES PRESS**

72 Fifth Avenue   3 Henrietta Street
NEW YORK, NY 10011 ● LONDON, WC2E 8LU

For information concerning workshops on staff Burn-out in the human services, please contact:

Jerry Edelwich, M.S.W.
100 Cold Spring Rd., #A514
Rocky Hill, CT 06067
203-529-9750

HV4l
· E33
cop. 2
0 0589389 3

Copyright © 1980 by Jerry Edelwich with Archie Brodsky

All rights reserved. No part of this work may be reproduced or utilized in any form or by any means, electronic or mechanical, including photocopying, microfilm and recording, or by any information storage and retrieval system without permission in writing from the publisher.

Printed in the United States of America
123456789   987654

Library of Congress Cataloging in Publication Data

Edelwich, Jerry.
  Burn-out.

  Bibliography: p. 251
  Includes index.
  1. Social workers.   2. Job satisfaction.
I. Brodsky, Archie, joint author.   II. Title.
HV41.E33   361.3'023   LC 79-27412
ISBN 0-87705-507-6   0-89885-035-5 (pbk)

For David, Michael, and Sarah

CONTENTS

ACKNOWLEDGMENTS

We are deeply, pleasurably, and gratefully indebted to Christina Edelwich, Sara and Stanley Bailis, Donald Pet, and Lee Silverstein, whose strong and constant support and beneficial influence have made this book much better than it might otherwise have been. They have been with us from beginning to end.

We also have enjoyed the loyal support and assistance of many other individuals, among whom we especially would like to thank Diane DuCharme, Janet Epp, Norma Fox, Donna Gertler, Herbert Getter, Peter Labbe, Ken Mikulski, Smokey Orcutt, David Powell, Diane Preice, Patti Putman, and Joanne Sullivan.

Most of all, we extend our thanks and appreciation to all those throughout the country whom we interviewed. Although we cannot acknowledge them by name, both because of their number and out of regard for their (and their clients') privacy, we will always be conscious of the magnitude of their contribution. We hope, as they do, that their candidly shared experiences will help make the experiences of others more fruitful and more satisfying.

J.E.

A.B.

Chapter 1

WHAT IS BURN-OUT?

What is Burn-out?

Staff Burn-out among professionals and paraprofessionals in the human services is much easier to observe and to describe than it is to define. It is many things, and many people. . . .

Burn-out is an overworked, underpaid drug addiction counselor, himself a recovering addict, drinking on the job until he has to resign because of an alcohol problem. Burn-out is high school teachers "bitching" about their students in the faculty lounge. Burn-out is a nurse feeling as if her "arms are being pulled out of their sockets" by all the patients who call for help as she walks past their rooms. Burn-out is a former priest, now a state employee, wondering why some of his alcoholic clients make three times as much money as he does. Burn-out is a college-educated Corrections Department worker bursting into tears upon hearing that an ex-inmate for whom she had found a job is back in prison. Burn-out is a hospital psychiatric ward experiencing complete staff turnover virtually every year. Burn-out is an indulgent supervisor giving a harried welfare case-worker Wednesday afternoons off at the state's expense.

Burn-out is an alcoholism counselor ducking out for a lunch break to get away from clients whose company he would have welcomed six months earlier. Burn-out is a social services administrator complaining about the federal government's "benign neglect" of his requests for increased funds for staff training. Burn-out is all of these people going about their jobs, putting in their hours, "not making waves." Burn-out is any one of them, when asked how he or she would feel about the prospect of doing the same job in the same place 10 years from now, replying, "I'd rather be dead."

Burn-out is the attitude that "a job is a job is a job." Or else it is—after however many months or years of stagnation, frustration, and apathy—no job at all.

These descriptions suggest a working definition. We can use the term "Burn-out" to refer to a progressive loss of idealism, energy, and purpose experienced by people in the helping professions as a result of the conditions of their work. Those conditions range from insufficient training to client overload, from too many hours to too little pay, from inadequate funding to ungrateful clients, from bureaucratic or political constraints to the inherent gap between aspiration and accomplishment. What we will try to do here is to suggest, through case studies and personal accounts, what Burn-out feels like, to isolate as many as possible of its common causes, to break down the process into stages of disillusionment that a person goes through, to understand how it affects people in different kinds of jobs and with different educational backgrounds—and, finally, to do something about it.

To the extent that individuals and institutions can recognize—better yet, anticipate—what Burn-out is and how, when, and where it occurs, they will be better prepared to resist the ineffectual, wishful remedies that are often practiced today and to seek more realistic antidotes. A positive approach to Burn-out will be based not on the hope of preventing it (which is virtually impossible), but on the realization that it will happen —perhaps repeatedly—in a person's career and must be dealt with on an ongoing basis. Burn-out can even be turned to advantage in that it can energize a person to break out of a rut. When frustration is used creatively, it becomes a stimulus to the kind of enthusiasm that it normally erodes.

WHY THE HELPING PROFESSIONS?

As an expression of human psychology and "human nature," Burn-out is, of course, not limited to work in the human services, or to any kind of work. Any kind of involvement that people form is vulnerable to doubt, disillusionment, and an eventual exhaustion of energy. Artists can suffer a creative Burn-out, lovers a burning out of passion. A study of Burn-out can be done in any profession. The physical symptoms of Burn-out that are commonly observed in human services personnel —ulcers, headaches, backaches, frequent colds, sexual problems—can just as easily be found in the high-pressure world of business. And yet, Burn-out does not occur with anything like the same regularity or carry with it the same social costs in business as it does in the human services, where it takes on a special character and a special intensity. Wherever people are working with people, the consequences of this thing that we call Burn-out are felt:

1. The idealistic expectations of the "helpers" are frustrated.
2. Services to clients are compromised.
3. Society, along with the social service institution, incurs high costs.

All three of these effects must be considered carefully by anyone who wants to understand and deal with Burn-out.

What is it about the helping professions that brings about these effects on such a large scale? Vocations in the human services are characterized by several built-in sources of frustration that eventually lead many dedicated workers to become ineffective and apathetic.

Noble Aspirations and High Initial Enthusiasm

Disillusioned idealism is different from disappointed ambition, and people who work in the human services, unlike most other fields, are susceptible to the former as well as the latter. The most often stated reason for coming into the field is the desire to help people. As we shall see in Chapter 3, the actual motivations are not always so simple, but they almost always include at least the belief that one wants to help. That this belief takes often extravagant and sometimes grandiose proportions is a function of our society's values. The aspiration for personal success alone, strong as it may be, must be kept within certain bounds of propriety, or else harbored secretly. But moral, altruistic ambitions have no limit; one may feel and express quite frankly the intention of doing good on a grand scale. The seeds of Burn-out are contained in the assumption that the real world will be in harmony with such dreams.

Lack of Criteria for Measuring Accomplishment

The gap between initial expectations and actual accomplishments in the human services would be large—and painful —enough for almost anyone without having the additional frustration of being unable to define just what constitutes accomplishment. How do people know whether they are doing a good job and whether anyone is benefiting from their services? People who come into the human services from "hard science" or "hard money" occupations (a common occurrence with alcoholics who become counselors after successful careers in business or technical fields) say that it is much more difficult to set standards for reviewing their own and others' performance in counseling than in their previous work. It is not always possible to quantify cure rates or, once quantified, to assess their implications. Time is a major issue here; how long is it reasonable to wait before expecting a client to show some progress? Another issue is lack of continuity in client–helper relationships;

if one's job is to treat acute problems and then refer clients to other facilities, how does one ever see, let alone evaluate, the results of one's labors?

Low Pay at All Levels of Education, Skill, and Responsibility

There is, of course, a range of pay scales as one goes up the educational ladder in the helping professions. But except at the highest levels, represented by psychiatrists and clinical psychologists (and sometimes even there), low pay is often a complaint. From the paraprofessional, "quasi-patient" drug addiction counselor who does not get a living wage to the social services adminstrator who is paid one-third or perhaps one-half as much as his or her counterpart in the private sector, the person who sets out to help others pays a price in economic well-being. So does that person's family, and the deprivations suffered by one's loved ones can have obvious personal and emotional repercussions. The disparity is painfully felt when one's old college classmates who went into business or law begin to display the trappings of a life-style that one cannot afford. Such sacrifices are willingly accepted by people who are really enthusiastic about what they are doing, but what happens when enthusiasm wanes? What happens when a person who does not earn enough to support a normal "outside life" begins to want one?

Upward Mobility Through the Administrative Channel

Most people look forward to improving their position in life through advancement in their careers. This desire will be strongly felt in a field where pay is lower than almost anywhere else and where hierarchical tensions and conflicts are no less present. That is to say, it is no more pleasant to be on the bottom in the human services than in any other occupation. However, the prospect of career advancement creates a dilemma for people who have come into the field because they want to help people. As they rise in pay and status, they find themselves getting farther away from the people they seek to serve. The nurse becomes head nurse of a ward; the teacher becomes department head or school principal; the drug counselor or corrections department worker becomes a supervisor whose job is no longer to provide direct services to clients, but to administer those who are providing the services. Once promoted, these individuals often find that they miss their patients, students, or clients, along with the satisfactions the job originally provided. They also miss their peers, who are transformed overnight from friends and comrades to mistrustful subordinates. "If I had wanted to be an administrator," they may ruefully reflect, "I wouldn't have gone into this field in the first place." But what if the alternative is to stay on in a powerless, low-paying position?

Sexism

Sexism is, of course, not limited to the human services. Nonetheless, this is an area where large numbers of nonclerical women staff workers are employed in positions of structured inferiority. Nurses are mostly women; doctors are mostly men. Family relations officers are mostly women; attorneys and judges are mostly men. Schoolteachers are mostly women; principals are mostly men. Sexual stereotyping influences job assignments, allocation of responsibilities, and standards of conduct on the job. Sexual polarization commonly reinforces polarization by rank and status. The chronically discontented nurses on a hospital ward may not be sure whether they resent the boss because he is a doctor or because he is a man.

Inadequate Funding and Institutional Support

The administrator who complained of "benign neglect" of his program by the powers-that-be was voicing a concern typical of those who work in private or governmental institutions that show a *pro forma* commitment to human services. Although needs tend to increase, funding at best levels off, especially when governments are under pressure to cut taxes and limit spending in "nonessential" areas. More often than not, funds are allocated according to the political requirements of the institution, as perceived by top management, rather than according to the needs of clients, as perceived by front-line workers who provide direct services. In funding as well as in other areas of policy, personnel from the bottom to the top of the administrative ladder see their recommendations disregarded and their decisions reversed or simply not acted upon at the next higher level. Nor are the institution's own stated principles likely to be reflected in practice. These are the facts of life in any large, hierarchical institution, whether it be a university, a hospital, or a state or federal agency.

Inefficient Use of Resources—the Dilemma of Case Management

In World War I the French Army Medical Corps developed a system of disaster medicine called *triage.* With battle casualties so numerous that the corps could not possibly attend to them all, the medics divided the wounded into three categories: (1) those who would die whether or not they received medical attention; (2) those who would survive whether or not they received medical attention; and (3) those would would die without medical attention, but who could be saved by timely care. Naturally, it was this third group that was given the most care. This classification system (with subsequent refinements) remains the basis of disaster medicine in both military and civilian facilities today. Although it appears callous and inhumane, it acknowledges the simple fact that where resources are limited (and where are they not?), humane ends are best served by using these resources where they will do some good.

This lesson has not been learned very well in the human services fields. It cannot be taught very explicitly, since it would be impolitic for, say, a state agency to announce that it is "abandoning" certain clients. Instead, it is publicly maintained that time and effort are apportioned fairly among all clients. This is what people coming into the field are led to believe, and as a result they expend their energies unwisely, trying to be all things to everyone. It is not unusual for a disproportionate amount of attention to be given to a small percentage of the population who simply will not respond to counseling. Considerable effort also goes into those who *do* respond—those who, because they are cooperative and do make progress, can be called "successes." What is lost in this concentration on the most frustrating and the most gratifying cases is the principle of triage (or, as it is called in the human services, *case management*): namely, to give attention to the people who are "on the fence," those for whom an intervention at the proper time might make a difference. New staff members, if they are fortunate, may be briefed informally on this concept by a supervisor who knows the score. More often, they learn it through hard experience.

High Public Visibility Coupled with Popular Misunderstanding and Suspicion

Although the puritan ethic is honored more in form than in deed by most twentieth-century Americans, most people nonetheless remain comfortable in their own hypocrisies when faced with drug addiction, crime, alcoholism, battered wives and children, and chronic poverty. They are mistrustful of people who are not like themselves, people who do not appear to be pulling their own weight, people for whose failings the taxpayer must foot the bill. The human services, moreover, are in a journalistic fishbowl, and the public understands as much about what the human services are as about any other subject that is susceptible to media sensation. The stories that reach the public eye and ear are not those of the constructive day-to-day work done in these areas, but of the occasional scandal, the dramatic recidivist, the abuse played up for shock value. As a result, people applaud the idea of a half-way house for exprison inmates or a residential treatment center for alcoholics—as long as it is in somebody else's neighborhood.

BURN-OUT: ITS NATURE, EXTENT, AND VARIATIONS

Burn-out occurs across the board, without regard to age, sex, discipline, or formal training. These distinctions do matter, but only insofar as they influence the specific forms that Burn-out can take. Chapter 6 describes a 12-point planning board exercise which, with minor modifications, can be given to anyone in the helping fields as a way of identifying significant sources of frustration. In this exercise, a person is asked to rank the following items in importance and to comment on their relevance to his or her situation:

not enough money
too many hours
career dead-end
too much paper work
not sufficiently trained for job
not appreciated by clients
not appreciated by supervisor
no support for important decisions
powerlessness
system not responsive to clients' needs
bad office politics

Along with these eleven items a blank piece of paper called the "Wild Card" is given out. Here the person is asked to write in any other major source of frustration that he or she faces. The items that turn up again and again as Wild Cards—e.g., sexism, too much travel, no social life, isolation from peers—can be used as part of the standard list where applicable. Taken together, the 12 points constitute the major sources of frustration that lead to Burn-out. Some of them have to do with the personal satisfactions and rewards that one gets from the job; others have to do with one's effectiveness in doing the job. Each of them is potentially applicable to anyone, but whether or not it does apply to a given individual often depends on that individual's background and the kind of position he or she holds.

Variations by Hierarchical Status Level

In the human services as elsewhere, the kinds of problems and preoccupations a person has on the job are in part determined by the person's place in the administrative hierarchy. Here we can identify three major categories:

1. *Front-line staff.* These are the people who provide services to clients directly. As such, they tend to be sympathetic to the needs of clients but may also feel unappreciated by them. Burdened by low pay and heavy case loads, they are often "eaten up" by the demands of clients on the one hand and supervisors on the other. Powerlessness is a major issue here. A typical complaint is: "Each client thinks he or she is the only person I have to attend to." Polarization between this group and administrators or high-status individuals in the same facilities (e.g., nurses versus doctors, psychiatric technicians versus psychiatrists) is common, with mutual ill will and frustration of effort.

2. *Middle management.* This is the staff supervisory level. Here the problem becomes one of balancing one's loyalties and defining and meeting one's commitments to those above and below in the hierarchy. The primary need at this level is to make one's influence count and to gain support for one's decisions.

3. *Top management.* The top administrators of a social service agency simultaneously play several roles—to-

ward clients, toward subordinates, toward superiors (e.g., government officials, foundation directors), and toward the public. Not only must they allocate authority within the institution, but they must also represent and defend the institution against what may be a hostile or suspicious community. They must protect their power base while accepting the publicity (within and outside the institution) that attends everything they do.

Variations by Educational Background and Job Description

The frustrations a person is susceptible to are not influenced solely by his or her position on the administrative ladder. They are affected as well by a broader set of determining factors, including the field in which one works, the kind of work one does, and the amount and kind of education one has had —which tie in again with the question of administrative responsibility. On the basis of the interviews and case studies cited throughout this book, we would suggest that virtually everyone working in the helping fields can be placed in one of the following occupational/educational categories:

1. *Paraprofessionals without formal training.* Paraprofessionals include addiction counselors with a background of substance abuse and/or imprisonment, welfare mothers working as casework assistants, and equally untrained individuals who serve as teachers' aides, nurses' aides, psychiatric technicians, or community service aides in police departments. The paraprofessional role is by its very nature a temporary one. There is too little pay, too much work, and too little power and status to satisfy anyone for very long. Those who attempt to build a life around a paraprofessional career face rapid disillusionment; the choice for the paraprofessional is whether to get more education

and better credentials or to leave the field. In the drug and alcohol fields, counselors who are themselves recovering addicts tend either to rise above the paraprofessional role through education or to return to substance abuse, with the latter group being in the majority.

2. *Young, college-educated idealists.* College graduates with bachelor's degrees in psychology, sociology, or the humanities sometimes seek jobs in the human services in the expectation of applying their academic training to working with people. Often they have as little formal training and status in the field as the paraprofessionals, though their education may give them alternative career choices. These well-intentioned individuals tend to overidentify with clients and otherwise betray a lack of experience to match their enthusiasm. They, too, face the choice of improving their credentials or meeting an impasse of ineffectiveness and frustration.

3. *Professionals with master's degrees (in education, psychology, or social work).* People who are adequately trained and fully qualified to work with people are still susceptible to the range of disillusioning factors that we have listed: namely, paperwork, heavy case load, bureaucratic hassles, staff polarization, etc. In particular, they face the great paradox that confronts people who enjoy working with people—the fact that upward mobility in the human services occurs primarily through the administrative channel and not through face-to-face dealings with clients.

4. *Professionals with doctorates (clinical psychologists and psychiatrists).* These high-status individuals enjoy good pay, job security, and a sense of security in their professional standing as well. The problems they face are those of overwork, isolation (if they are in private practice), doubts about the value of their work, and resulting family and health problems.

5. *Top administrators.* The directors of programs and agencies—at least those who rise from the ranks (as most do) rather than being career administrators—face a special variant of a typical frustration in the helping professions: that of not being adequately trained for their jobs. They have been trained to help people, whether as social workers, psychologists, or psychiatrists. Having done this job well, they are elevated to a position where they must do things they have *not* been trained to do: that is, administer staff, conduct public relations, and negotiate the byzantine pathways of public and private bureaucracy.

These distinctions will be highlighted throughout our interviews. It should be noted, though, that a person can move from one category to another, primarily through further education. Such movement can be one of the most effective interventions for Burn-out, provided that it is accompanied by the realization that change brings new problems as well as satisfactions.

DYNAMICS OF CONTAGION

If Burn-out only affected individuals in isolation, it would be far less important and far less devastating in its impact than it is. Burn-out in human services agencies is like staph infection in hospitals: it gets around. It spreads from clients to staff, from one staff member to another, and (most crucially) from staff back to clients. Perhaps it ought to be called "staff infection."

The spread of Burn-out is a matter of socialization, in both senses of the word. When staff members socialize with clients, they can easily be drawn into an emotional identification with clients and an involvement in the clients' value system. When staff members socialize with one another on the job, or when human services professionals limit their outside social contacts to other people in the same field, they may be socialized into a set of values involving overdedication on the one hand or cynicism on the other, either of which leaves them susceptible to Burn-out. The key concept here is William Glasser's idea of the "small world," in this case the world of the job, that becomes the sole source of a person's values and satisfactions.

The currents of progressive disillusionment—of enthusiasm, stagnation, frustration, and apathy—run in all of the following directions.

From Clients to Staff

We see Burn-out in a nutshell when a dedicated but inexperienced counselor bursts into tears because a client is back on drugs or back in jail. The vicarious involvement in clients' lives produces overidentification, unrealistic expectations, and finally a painful letdown.

From Staff to Staff

New, inexperienced staff members are coopted by senior staff members into the values by which an institution is informally run—especially if the new staff members have new and threatening ideas about how things should be run. Expressions like "What are you knocking yourself out for?" and "You'll never beat the system" serve to keep the new person in line and preserve the existing order of things. Discouragement deepens when staff members, instead of developing independent friendships and family lives, go out drinking together after work and talk about the difficulties and disappointments of the day.

From Staff to Clients

A counselor in one of the military services once remarked, "People say, 'The clients are burning me out.' But really it's the other way around." When the "helpers" are discouraged, they do not work as hard or as effectively, and they do not do as good a job for their clients. Clients pick this up; they know when they are getting the runaround. The negative effect on client morale is one of the most serious consequences of Burn-out, for it defeats the entire purpose of the individual helper and the helping agency.

Ironically, given that the human services are built upon the concept of involvement, it takes a degree of detachment to control the contagion of Burn-out. The novice counselor who no longer cries over each instance of recidivism is giving up a bit of idealism, but also is learning to work more effectively. Professional maturity is to a great extent a question of knowing when to be involved and when to be detached. One of the key interventions for Burn-out is the creation of an "outside life" —family, friends, interests, activities—that keeps one's whole being from being wrapped up in the job.

STAGES OF DISILLUSIONMENT

The portrait of Burn-out to be drawn in this book comes from interviews with people who have worked in the human services in many different capacities and in an equally wide range of settings. The experiences of these individuals are presented as they have felt and described them, without endorsement of their political, economic, or sociological explanations of the stresses they have felt. Burn-out is a fact of life, one that exists for any number of reasons and that must be dealt with.

These are not extreme cases. Very few of them involve people who have left the field altogether (although many have changed jobs within the field a number of times). The tensions and disappointments revealed here are those that exist between the lines of people's lives. Often, therefore, they are only revealed in subtle ways, as when a counselor working with prison inmates talks about recidivists coming back to jail "again and again and again," tapping out the rhythm of his frustration on the table as he speaks; or when a middle-aged alcoholism counselor, himself not that long into recovery, slips into referring to the line of "wall-to-wall alcoholics" he must see daily as "these people."

What emerges from the interviews and from long observation and experience in the field is a picture of a process of disillusionment that commonly occurs in the following stages, each of which (following a chapter on the development of the concept of Burn-out) forms one or more chapters of this book. Within each stage the chapter divisions simply indicate different aspects of the stage in question.

Enthusiasm

This is the initial period of high hopes, high energy, and unrealistic expectations, when one does not yet know what the job is all about (see Chapter 3). It is when one does not need anything in life but the job, because the job promises to be everything. Overidentification with clients and excessive and inefficient expenditure of one's own energy (including voluntary overwork) are major hazards of this stage.

Stagnation

Here one is still doing the job, but the job is no longer so thrilling as to substitute for everything else in life (see Chapters 4 and 5). Enough of the reality has come through to make one feel that it might be nice to have leisure time, a little money to spend, a car, some friends, a lover, a family, a home. The emphasis now is on meeting one's own personal needs, and the issues of money, working hours, and career development now become important.

Frustration

At this point one calls into question one's effectiveness in doing the job and the value of the job itself (see Chapters 6–8). What is the point of trying to help people when they do not respond? What is the point of trying to help people when "the bureaucracy" frustrates one's best efforts? The limitations of the job situation are now viewed not simply as detracting from one's personal satisfaction and status, but as threatening to defeat the purpose of what one is doing. Emotional, physical, and behavioral problems can occur at this stage.

Apathy

This is the typical and very natural defense mechanism against frustration (see Chapter 9). It occurs when a person is chronically frustrated on the job, yet needs the job to survive. Apathy is the attitude that "a job is a job is a job." It means putting in the minimum required time (as against the overtime that is gladly undertaken during the stage of enthusiasm), avoiding challenges (even avoiding *clients* whenever possible), and seeking mainly to keep from endangering the secure position that compensates, however, inadequately, for the loss of job satisfaction.

Intervention

Intervention is whatever is done in response to or in anticipation of enthusiasm, stagnation, frustration, or apathy (see Chapters 10 and 11). Intervention breaks the cycle. It may mean leaving the field or changing jobs within the field. It may mean modifying one's job description and restructuring one's relations with clients, subordinates, peers, and superiors. It may mean going back to school to obtain better credentials, or just to stimulate one's interest and curiosity. It may mean expanding one's life outside the job. It may mean taking a vacation, arranging for more time off, or moving out of a residential facility. It may mean simply looking around for the nearest "workshop high." Obviously, some interventions are more effective than others in the long run, and the trick is to find the ones that produce lasting change.

There are two things to bear in mind about this cycle.

First, it is highly contagious. If the counselor is enthusiastic, the clients are enthusiastic. If the teacher stagnates, the students stagnate. If the nurse is frustrated, the patients are frustrated. If a trainer/supervisor is apathetic, he or she will produce apathetic social workers.

Second, the progression is not linear and not inevitable. Rather, it is cyclic; it can repeat itself any number of times. The same person may go through the complete Burn-out cycle several times in different jobs, or even in the same job. On the hopeful side, the cycle can be interrupted by a decisive intervention at any point (although it is much harder to break through apathy than stagnation or frustration).

Intervention is the major thrust of this book. Just as intervention can occur at any of the stages of Burn-out, so each chapter includes some illustrations of how individuals cope with the problems commonly encountered in a given stage. The most broadly useful methods of coping, those derived from William Glasser's Reality Therapy and Albert Ellis's Rational-Emotive Therapy, are those that work from an acknowledgment of existing conditions rather than an idealized reconstruction of the helping relationship, social service institutions, or society as a whole.

Our overall purpose is to explore, at both the individual and institutional levels, which interventions are meaningful and which are trivial, and how one can go about intervening in a way that matters. For the institution, the goal is to develop training strategies that will prepare people more effectively for Burn-out, both for their own benefit and to reduce the costs incurred by the institution. For the individual, the goal is to accept reality, to assume responsibility for oneself, and to be able to derive enjoyment and a sense of self-worth from doing a job that is worth doing well.

Chapter 2

RECOGNITION AND SCOPE OF THE PROBLEM

The costs of Burn-out in staff turnover do not have to be documented statistically; any social services administrator knows them well. Every year, fields such as nursing, teaching, and social work suffer the loss of hundreds of their most dedicated and sensitive practitioners to occupational battle fatigue. The hardy soul who lasts out five years on the staff of a hospital psychiatric ward or drug rehabilitation program may well see as many as three complete cycles of turnover in personnel (including top administrators). The costs of staff turnover are felt by clients, fellow staff members, the institution, and society. These costs include the sizeable financial expense of training new staff, the disruption of client services with the loss in continuity of client–staff relationships, and the lowering of staff morale. The destructive impact on morale reflects the fact that turnover is not only a result of Burn-out, but a cause of Burn-out as well. In many social service milieux, peer solidarity and support (including "on-the-job training" and informal supervision by peers) are essential for what is often an understaffed facility with undertrained personnel to do its job adequately.

Out of dire necessity, a community of peers arises. When some staff members become discouraged or worn out and resign, to be replaced (if at all) by inexperienced strangers, the community is fragmented, causing the remaining staff members to lose a vital source of support. This peer support is regained only when the community reconstructs itself around the newcomers, and not everyone has the strength to hang on until that happens.

FORMAL AND INFORMAL RECOGNITION

Despite the prevalence of this "vicious cycle" in virtually every setting where people are helping people, and despite the fact that Burn-out and its causes can in retrospect be seen clearly in many older accounts of the human services professions (such as Stanton and Schwartz's[1] classic study of the sociology of a mental institution), there has until recent years been no formal recognition of Burn-out in the human services literature. At the level of informal recognition, the story has been different. What counselor or social worker has not been to one of those weekend workshops which have the stated purpose of teaching job skills and the unstated purpose of reinvigorating dispirited "helpers"? Who has not felt the "workshop high" that comes from getting away from the stress of the job and airing one's doubts and problems among a new group of people? Who has not felt that "high" dissipate in the weeks following the return to the job, as it becomes clear that nothing has really changed? This approach to dealing with Burn-out without giving it a name becomes a large budgetary item in many help-giving institutions. Its effects are temporary and superficial, like those of any other "fix."

By 1980 many of these workshops, constructive and otherwise, have come to be explicitly concerned with Burn-out. People who always knew they had a problem can now give it a name. There are signs that the occupational hazard of human services personnel is becoming the latest "fad disease," a label that individuals willingly pin on themselves like a name tag on their hospital whites. At the other extreme is the supervisor who sadly pronounces everyone on the staff except himself to be burned out. "These are our worst cases of Burn-out, Doc," he will say. "Better get them to the emergency room right away." When we look at these extremes of self-dramatization and self-deception, we may wonder whether this kind of recognition of the problem is worse than no recognition at all.

Although Burn-out undoubtedly has always occurred and will always occur, it is not surprising that people have become conscious of it—and given it a name—in the 1970s. Although the strain on the individual worker was just as great in the 1960s as it is today, enthusiasm probably lasted longer when there was a hopeful sense that society supported the idea of helping the less fortunate. That commitment was backed up by increased outlays of funds which made the human services an expanding enterprise. Today, with those funds being reclaimed for the private sector, the enthusiasm of the 1960s has burned out. For on top of the concrete practical difficulties created by reductions in funding, the very idea of a "taxpayers' revolt" against human services funding is necessarily dispiriting to those who staff the agencies under attack.

State workers who feel that they work too much and are paid too little are now being told that (according to the "Proposition 13 mentality") they work too little and are paid too much. If society does not appreciate what they are doing, they understandably feel, why should they expend energy and make sacrifices to get the job done? Still, the job is getting done and must continue to get done, more or less. But it must get done more cheaply and efficiently (e.g., with less turnover in personnel). Thus, institutions as well as individuals have had all the more reason to develop an understanding of Burn-out and its antidotes that goes beyond the "workshop high."

From the Particular to the Universal

The word "Burn-out" came into the professional literature in 1974 with the first of psychoanalyst Herbert J. Freudenberger's[2] articles on staff Burn-out in "alternative" help-giving facilities, such as free clinics, that exist outside the established institutional structures of society and that depend on dedicated volunteer help. It soon was recognized that the concept applied equally well to the salaried or self-employed professional in an "establishment" position: the psychiatrist in private practice, the nurse in a centercity hospital, the director of a state college counseling program. More recent articles have addressed themselves to Burn-out in teachers,[3] police officers,[4] lawyers,[5] nurses,[6] mental health workers,[7] and day care staff.[8]

As the history of research and writing on the subject suggests, Burn-out initially was associated with "front-line" clinical settings (such as crisis centers and drug and alcohol rehabilitation programs) where undertrained workers put in long hours providing direct services for an overload of clients. Burn-out was easiest to observe in such settings because its effects were most readily apparent there. If that were all there was to Burn-out, however, there would not be so many psychiatrists who commit suicide, so many physicians who develop a Demerol habit, so many well-paid helping professionals who are at risk of migraine headaches, ulcers, excessive smoking, broken marriages, emotional trauma, and other symptoms of unrelieved emotional pressure. An article in *Psychiatric Opinion* on "The professional burnout syndrome"[9] represents just one more addition to the extensive literature on, for example, narcotic addiction and mental disorders among physicians.[10]

Professional training works for many people as a remedy for some causes of Burn-out because it offers increased knowledge (in the form of supervised field experience) together with greater status, power, and autonomy and a wider range of opportunities. But it is no sure cure. If a volunteer manning a

suicide hotline faces the dilemma of having been given a mandate to do a job without the resources to carry it out, so does
a psychiatrist at a state-run mental hospital. The human services administrator who never quite knows what his job is
because each new boss requires that he interpret it differently
is subject to much the same anxiety and disorientation as the
front-line worker to whom the contradictory directives ultimately filter down.

Burn-out has causes that go deeper than long hours, low
pay, insufficient training, and hierarchical subordination. A
person who makes a vocation of helping others exposes his or
her own vulnerability in a number of ways. There is the "there
but for the grace of God go I" reaction, whereby the client
becomes a disturbing mirror image of the helper's real or potential suffering ("You see your own craziness in the patient, and
you defend against it by withdrawing behind your authority").
There is the helper's need to be needed, or as one therapist put
it, "You want to be needed and wanted, but not completely
responsible for a person." And then, as if to show how pro-
foundly difficult it is *not* to hold oneself responsible, there is the
giving of oneself, the sharing of pain, that a caring person
experiences. Every time the wounds cannot be healed or the
suffering alleviated, it becomes harder to open oneself again to
another's pain.

One of the reasons people seek to help others (and it is not
a disreputable motive) is to confirm their sense of their own
power—not necessarily power over others, but simply some
noticeable impact on the world. Burn-out, in its most general
and universal sense, occurs when this wish is frustrated,
whether because of the mundane bureaucratic obstacles to
effective treatment, the projection of the helper's own feelings
and needs onto the client's situation, or the inherent difficulty
of changing what another person does and is. It occurs when
one sets out to move the world a bit, only to find oneself with
the world pressing down on one's shoulders.

Present and Future Directions

Although in a field as new as Burn-out a review of literature is likely to become obsolete almost as soon as it is published, one cannot write about this subject without acknowledging the major contribution made by two social psychologists at the University of California at Berkeley, Christina Maslach and Ayala Pines. In addition to their articles (cited above) on Burn-out in specific occupational categories, they have broadened the concept so as to make clear its implications for anyone who works with people in a helping role. Maslach has written several articles on Burn-out in the helping professions generally.[11] For research and diagnostic purposes she has developed (with Susan E. Jackson) the Maslach Burn-out Inventory, a questionnaire which measures four dimensions of Burn-out: emotional exhaustion, negative attitudes toward recipients, negative self-evaluation as a helper, and emotional distance from recipients.[12] Pines, in a particularly informative study of "occupational tedium" co-authored by Ditsa Kafry, gives a comprehensive picture of the emotional and institutional realities affecting those who work in the social services, ranging from overinvolvement of the ego to "large amounts of paperwork, low salaries, poor relationships with agency administrators, poor supervision and leadership, and bureaucratic inertia."[13] A noteworthy finding concerned the value subjects assigned to various work activities:[14]

> The highest mean values for satisfaction were for direct contact with clients and interaction with co-workers. The lowest mean value was for paperwork, an activity that also received the highest mean value for the amount of time the respondents actually devoted to it. The second lowest mean value for satisfaction was for administrative duties, an activity that ranked second highest in the mean time devoted to it.

As will be shown in subsequent chapters, these preferences are consistent with those revealed by the present authors' observations and interviews.

There are other areas in which our findings raise questions about some of the standard explanations and prescriptions in the existing literature on Burn-out. On the following questions the present work takes a somewhat different emphasis from that of other observers. The difference, however, is one of degree, and the questions remain questions. It is hoped that they will point the way to further refinements of our understanding of Burn-out.

1. *When is detachment part of the problem, and when is it part of the solution?* Detachment from clients is such a basic part of Burn-out that it is sometimes taken to be synonymous with the Burn-out syndrome itself. In our own scheme a pronounced emotional withdrawal is recognized to be a sign of the final stage of apathy. At the same time, as Maslach and Pines make clear in their allusions to "detached concern," a healthy degree of detachment can help save a person from severe Burn-out. It is part of an overall professionalism that increases therapeutic effectiveness and minimizes the psychological consequences of failure. Care should be taken not to use the term Burn-out as a pejorative label for kinds of detachment that actually represent sensible triage decisions, such as limiting the time spent with hopelessly unresponsive clients.

2. *When does "ventilation" become "bitching"?* Most commentaries stress the need for social support systems on the job to give workers an outlet for ventilating frustration. It is thought that this mutual support will prevent individual workers from thinking themselves alone in their problems and perhaps blaming themselves as well. As we will see in the stage of stagnation, however, workers in many fields already give one another such support through informal

"bitching" sessions. Those who write as if excessive alcohol use were the only danger of such sessions are ignoring another danger—that of Burn-out becoming a contagion. Workers are socialized into feeling burned out in the sobriety of the teachers' lounge as well as in the after-hours bar. If ventilation is going to be sanctioned as part of the institutional work day, therefore, the question is how to structure it so as to keep it constructive.

3. *Is time away from clients the answer?* People who work in any stressful occupation do need to take breaks from the most draining aspects of their work. Just as Maslach distinguishes between "sanctioned time-outs" and irresponsible "escapes" that leave clients unattended, so we will speak of "legitimated malingering" as an unproductive intervention that can be as damaging to the helper as to the client. It is certainly helpful (within budgetary limitations) to build some less intense catch-up time into a worker's schedule. But before unreservedly recommending paperwork and administration to fill up such break time, we should be aware that the near-universal complaint of human services workers is not too much time spent with clients, but too much paper work, which keeps them away from clients. Those who "escape into administration" usually are escaping not from direct service roles (which they give up with considerable internal conflict and regret), but from insufficient pay, status, and power.

4. *Is it possible or desirable to prevent Burn-out?* The idea of Burn-out has become controversial in some quarters where it has been taken to mean that a counselor or other helping professional can only work for a few years before leaving the field. This melodramatic extension of the concept has kept some institutions from acknowledging and coping with Burn-out. Maslach and Pines' effort to intervene in the situational

factors affecting Burn-out while conceding that there are no universal solutions is certainly a more constructive approach. We would also like to suggest a middle course, which is to say that although Burn-out will always occur, and although it may be useless to try to prevent it, individuals and organizations can still learn to manage it consciously and use it as a source of creative energy. One cannot smooth out the surf, but one can ride the waves—if one sees them coming.

5. *Is Burn-out best attacked at the organizational or individual level?* Since staff members would not get so frustrated if institutions and clients did not do such frustrating things, there is a natural impulse to try to change the way organizations are structured or the way clients behave. But that is a very big "if." Maslach,[15] for example, concludes a discussion of staff–client relations with recommendations such as the following:

> One implication of the earlier analysis of the client's dependent stance is that any efforts to make clients more self-reliant would have beneficial consequences for both clients and staff alike. For one thing, if clients took a more active and initiating role in their interactions with staff, the relationship could come closer to being one between equals. Staff and clients could function more as partners in the resolution of a problem and share in the responsibility for the decisions made. Clients would find their role less demeaning, and staff would find theirs less of an emotional burden. To the extent that clients are encouraged to be more independent and take responsibility for various aspects of the intervention, the frequently overworked staff would be relieved of some of their duties. Although such a change might be an enormous undertaking, involving as it does a resocialization of both clients and staff, it would do much to ease the emotional stresses that are currently a common part of staff–client contact.

It would be such an enormous undertaking that it is hard to imagine more than a very small percentage of

the people reading this passage being able to put it to any practical use. The helping professions exist in part for the purpose of resocializing clients; the Burn-out syndrome itself testifies to the difficulty of doing so. It is not clear why it would be any easier to resocialize clients for the good of the helping relationship than for their own good.

Perhaps the readership of scholars and administrators that Maslach addresses in the article just cited will include some who can apply her suggestions so as to revolutionize or significantly reform the helping professions. But for the worker in the field those suggestions have the ring of theoretically sound conclusions that remain abstract and speculative when measured against the exigencies of daily work. Since the present work (like some of Maslach's other writings) is intended primarily for the staff member experiencing. Burn-out rather than for an academic readership, it proceeds from the assumption that clients and the organization will go on being what they are, and that it is up to the individual worker to do what he or she can within those parameters.

OTHER PERSPECTIVES

Although the literature on organizational psychology may not have much to say to the individual staff member, the potentially valuable perspective it offers for understanding and dealing with Burn-out at the administrative level should not be overlooked. The question of job satisfaction, a relatively recent concern in the human services, has preoccupied managers in the private sector for a good part of the twentieth century. The "human relations" school of management has produced a vast literature on such questions as the social–psychological dynamics of work organizations, the nature and varieties of managerial authority, the value of worker participation in decision making, the relative importance of various forms of job satisfaction (pay, recognition, autonomy, creativity, etc.) in increasing worker motivation, and the ways in which organizational structure, job satisfaction, and productivity are related to one another.[16]

Business and industry have supported such research because its benefits (in efficiency and productivity) are seen as exceeding its costs. As the costs of Burn-out in the human services become more apparent, the alternative of enlightened management will become more attractive. The budgetary squeeze felt in the wake of the "Proposition 13 mentality," by putting pressure on human service organizations to manage themselves in a business-like, cost-conscious manner, has led public and private help-giving agencies to begin to look to organizational behavior consultants and their writings for managerial guidance. A straw in the wind is an article on organizational remedies for Burn-out written by the leading organizational psychologist Robert Kahn.[17] (His recommendations will be discussed in Chapter 11.)

Another, very different area of professional literature which bears upon Burn-out is concerned with effectiveness in counseling and other helping relationships. A growing body of research has shown that regardless of the type of helping relationship (psychotherapy, social work, teaching, etc.), regardless of the discipline in which the helper has been trained (Freudian, behaviorist, etc.), and regardless of the type of client (alcoholic, schizophrenic, delinquent, etc.), a person who has certain key character traits will be an effective counselor, whereas one who does not have those traits will be ineffective.[18] Psychologist Sidney Wolf[19] lists ten dimensions of effectiveness in interpersonal relations:

> *empathy*—"the ability to perceive accurately what another person is experiencing and to communicate that perception"
> *respect*—appreciation of "the dignity and worth of another human being," and of that person's right to make his or her own choices in his or her own time
> *genuineness*—"the ability of an individual to be freely and deeply himself"
> *concreteness*—"specificity of expression concerning the client's feelings and experiences"

confrontation—the capacity to challenge the client on discrepancies in his or her statements, feelings, and actions

self-disclosure—"the revealing of personal feelings, attitudes, opinions, and experiences on the part of the therapist for the benefit of the client"

immediacy—the ability to deal with "the feeling between the client and the counselor in the here and now"

warmth—the expression of verbal and nonverbal concern and affection

potency—"the dynamic force and magnetic quality of the therapist"

self-actualization—the capacity to "live and meet life directly," to be "effective at living"

Seen as personality traits, none of these can be taught. Seen as counseling skills, all of them can be taught. That is, one cannot be trained to be empathic, but one can be trained to give empathic responses. One cannot be trained to be warm or to be concrete; one can be trained to manifest warmth or concreteness.

What do these traits have to do with Burn-out? By themselves they will not prevent Burn-out. A person can have all of these traits, be an effective helper, and still burn out. Nonetheless, the confidence and the demonstrated effectiveness that come from possessing these traits in some degree (and in greater degree as one gains experience) are about the best anchoring that one can have in a field where one must cope with the unpredictable behavior of clients, colleagues, and institutions. These basic counseling skills are the core of the professional training that can be a partial insulation against Burn-out.

THE FIVE-STAGE SYSTEM

The approach to Burn-out that this book will take, which divides the process into stages of enthusiasm, stagnation, frustration, apathy, and intervention, was developed by the senior author before he ever heard the word "Burn-out." It came out of his observation of the extremely high rates of turnover among state-employed paraprofessionals and of recidivism among "recovering" or "drug-free" addiction counselors in the early 1970s. When he began to share these observations with classes in counseling, the students let him know that the problem was not limited to former substance abusers or even to paraprofessionals, but was pervasive in the helping professions.

As he broadened the scope of his observations, the author found that the many specific discontents and career trajectories of individuals in different helping fields could be subsumed under the stages presented here. Speaking before diverse groups about what he then still referred to simply as "Stages of Disillusionment in the Helping Professions," he saw the idea elicit reactions of unexpected intensity and poignancy. Whatever the type of helping agency involved, the staff members thought he was speaking directly to them.

When staff Burn-out became a common topic of discussion in the human services in the middle and late years of the decade, its close relationship to the scheme the author had developed was apparent. Out of the 12-point planning board exercise grew the author's workshops, which in turn (along with personal experience, collegial discussion, teaching, and interviewing) gave rise to other concepts and coping strategies presented here. But the distinguishing feature of this model of Burn-out remains the original five-stage sequence. It is in terms of these five stages that Burn-out will be discussed in the following chapters.

Chapter 3

IDEALISTIC ENTHUSIASM

When people in the helping professions are asked to recall what they felt during their first weeks on the job—what they expected the job to be like, what they hoped to accomplish—they give answers like these:

> A recovering alcoholic in his 50s working in a hospital detox unit: "I was going to be the Martin Luther King of the drunks, leading them all to the promised land."
>
> A social worker in a state welfare department: "I was full of new ideas for people that, I thought, would make their lives infinitely better."
>
> A high-ranking Naval enlisted man counseling enlistees referred for disciplinary problems: "I felt that everyone would leave my office happy, healthy, and wise."
>
> A high school English teacher: "I expected to raise everyone's reading proficiency by three grade levels."
>
> A family counselor in private practice who entered the field in her thirties after a successful career in corporate administration: "I had a God-like view of what I could give people."

An officer at a reformatory for young women: "I was simply going to undo all the wrongs done by society over hundreds of years."

A correctional counselor with master's degrees in sociology and public administration: "I saw myself as an instrument of change in the Department of Corrections and in the inmates' lives. I thought I'd be able to turn people around from a criminal life style to a straight-arrow existence."

A drug rehabilitation counselor in a therapeutic community: "I was on my white horse, spreading the gospel of mental health and the evils of addiction. I pictured myself doing group therapy in Yankee Stadium, curing 50,000 people at a time."

The director of a regional center for alcoholism treatment: "I wanted to build an empire, a comprehensive service program for alcoholics and their families."

These recollections dramatize what the initial stage of *enthusiasm* feels like to the enthusiast. In many of them there can be detected a note of bitter hyperbole, of self-parody; a rueful acknowledgment that things had not turned out quite as envisioned. When the individuals quoted were interviewed, years had passed since they had experienced the emotions they sought to articulate. In that time (indeed, in most cases within six months on the job) reality had intervened. A psychiatric technician who had been working for a year in a hospital psychiatric unit had to be reminded (by a co-worker who had decided to leave the unit) how enthusiastic he himself had originally been. "This guy told me how different I had been, how much I had changed," he related. "I'd forgotten what I was like back then."

Sentiments like those expressed in the quotations above are bound to fall victim to reality. The schoolteacher who wanted to "raise everyone's reading proficiency by three grade levels" soon found her aspirations scaled down to "keeping the students interested for 15 minutes at a time." Much of what we know as Burn-out stems from this discrepancy between expectation and reality. It is for this reason that enthusiasm calls for intervention every bit as much as do stagnation, frustration, and apathy. Unlike these later stages of Burn-out, enthusiasm feels good and looks good at the time. Being contagious, it even leads to good outcomes for clients in some cases. But it also leads to Burn-out for the counselor.

Intervention may be difficult at the stage of enthusiasm for the simple reason that it is hard to help people who do not realize they have a problem. On the other hand, it is most productive to reach people at a time when they have not gone very far down the road to disillusionment and when they still have a good deal of energy to put into their work. Interventions for enthusiasm are best made in training, so that trainees can learn to moderate their expectations before they go out into the field. Such interventions require an awareness of how and why unrealistic hopes arise and just what is unrealistic about them.

What commonly are the expectations of a person entering the human services field? Why do novice "helpers" almost always have the same sorts of expectations? The question suggests another: What kind of person enters the human services field in the first place?

WHY PEOPLE BECOME HELPERS

People go into the human services to make a living, but not to make money. Although the full extent of the inequities in payment between publicly funded human services positions and jobs in the private sector may only become apparent after a person has invested years of training and work in a "helping" vocation, there is a general awareness that such vocations do not pay especially well. A psychiatrist or clinical psychologist can anticipate earning a substantial income, but there are usually other, equally important motivations for entering one of these professions. One psychiatrist, who takes time from his private practice to direct a state-funded addiction treatment center, puts it this way: "Money is important to me, but if working for the state enables me to do something interesting, I'll accept a reduction of income." His sentiments are echoed by people at all levels of income and professional attainment in the human services, who say that the kind of work they are doing is more important than what they are paid for it. Once the work itself ceases to be satisfying, however, money does become an issue, as will be shown in Chapter 5.

Job security is sometimes mentioned as a reason for entering the field, particularly by those who hold civil service positions. Indeed, the very fact that the medical, psychological, and social problems of human beings are not about to disappear is attractive to the individual who seeks guaranteed employment. "They'll always need nurses," explained one woman—a forecast which not long ago applied to teachers as well. Increasingly, however, it is job insecurity that characterizes most human services fields, since these tend to be the first to feel the effects of government budget cuts. In any case, job security is not one of the most prominently mentioned reasons for undertaking a career in the helping professions.

Avowed and Unavowed Motives

The motivation that virtually everyone in the field "owns up to" is the desire to help people. This is the major *avowed* reason for going into the field, and in most cases it is undoubtedly a sincere one. People become "helpers" because they really enjoy working with people and want to make a difference in people's lives. Those who are genuinely involved, at least at the outset, far outnumber those who are cynical and self-seeking.

Nonetheless, although the helping relationship focuses on the needs of the person to whom help is given, the needs of the helper come into play as well. At one level there are the helper's needs as a helper (e.g., the need to be needed). Then there are the helper's needs as a person, which can be touched off by the natural impulse to identify with the people one cares for. Thus, the avowed reason for going into the field masks two *unavowed* reasons that are equally salient: (1) the desire to learn about oneself, and (2) the desire to exert control. Again, this does not mean that most people are insincere when they say that they want to help others. Rather, it means that many people want to help others because, unbeknownst to themselves, they see it as a way of achieving one or both of these latent aims.

For many workers in the field, professional or paraprofessional involvement with people is a kind of self-exploration. It may be an unofficial, perhaps unacknowledged extension of one's own psychotherapy or a quasi-therapeutic attempt to come to terms with unresolved emotional conflicts. This self-projection into the helping relationship is more evident in the lower strata of professional training—for instance, among drug and alcohol counselors who, as recovering substance abusers, are regarded as patients themselves. But it occurs across the board. It may take the form of countertransference, whereby one views a client as a important "other" in one's own life. At its worst, this extraprofessional involvement in the helping relationship causes the counselor's needs to take precedence over the client's. It causes one to be impatient with and intolerant of clients who do not respond quickly enough. These consequences will be examined more closely in considering the problem of overidentification.

One way of avoiding such negative effects is by having some awareness of one's own motivations. The desire to learn about oneself and to work through one's emotional problems is not necessarily an obstacle to good counseling. It can, in fact, be a source of positive motivation, energy, and empathy. But this outcome is more likely to occur when one is aware (as many counselors are) that one's own needs are a factor in one's involvement with others. Members of Alcoholics Anonymous who become professional counselors as an extension of 12-step work do so with the consciously expressed intention of solidifying their own recovery by helping others. A young counselor in a state corrections department offered these reflections about his early days on the job:

> If I perceived a great enough need, I would do practically any-
> thing for the inmates. But whose need was I perceiving? In all
> likelihood, my own as much as theirs. I had a real need to be
> liked, to be understood, to be a part of what was going on in their
> lives.

Starting out from that kind of awareness, one can use one's
emotional investment in the job as the basis for insight rather
than an acting out of one's own emotional imperatives at the
expense of clients.

The need to exert control over others also may stem from
countertransference, in that it may reflect a need to change the
behavior of a recalcitrant self or other. It is, however, too basic
a human drive to require any special explanation. Among people who choose the human services as a vocation, the desire for
control is most likely to be acknowledged as a motivating factor
by those who aspire to administrative posts—to the extent that
it is acknowledged at all. For understandable reasons, people
are less aware of or less candid about this motivation than about
that of wanting to learn about themselves. Beneath the surface
of altruism, however, it is very much there—in the teacher's
power over students "once the classroom door is closed," in the
psychiatrist's capacity to mobilize and focus a client's emotions,
in the very nature and structure of the helping relationship. It
is part of the seductive appeal of the human services career for
many individuals. When gratified, it can be dangerous to the
client. When frustrated, it can be dangerous to the counselor,
since the eventual realization that one does not have very much
control over clients, the institution, and "the system" is a major
contributor to Burn-out.

Taken together, the chance to explore one's own deepest
feelings and the prospect of influencing the behavior of others
are like a powerful drug acting on latent wishes for self-aggrandizement. In this sense, setting out to work with people instead
of with things can be a heady experience. Thus the inflated
rhetoric of the somewhat embarrassed reminiscences with
which this chapter began.

Career Models and Client/Student Expectations

An important factor in bringing people into the human services is the example of others. People want to be like the people who have helped them. Such emulation is especially common in teaching and medicine, since every young person is exposed to teachers and doctors, and some of these prove to be inspiring models. In other human services fields, the experience of being a client often engenders the desire to be a helper. A state welfare caseworker, when asked why she chose that line of work, said, "My family was poor, and I know what it means to be given a hand. I want to help others as others helped me." A woman in her mid-30s, who had never previously considered a career in human services, sought assistance with her own family problems at a family relations institute. As she later reported, "I was fascinated by the idea that, with proper assistance, people really can make changes. I saw how much constructive work there was to do in the 'people fields.' " As a result, she went back to school and became a family counselor herself.

The experience of having been helped provides perhaps the strongest possible demonstration of the value of helping. At the same time, it creates expectations of what it will be like to assume the role of helper. People who have been counseled unsuccessfully do not become counselors. The people who become counselors are those who have been counseled successfully, and their experiences as cooperative clients who have benefited from the services offered them may give them unrealistic expectations. They may expect all clients to be as receptive and resourceful as they themselves were, and all counselors to be as competent and caring as those who counseled them.

Another source of skewed or misshapen expectations is one's experience as a student in a human services training program. A dedicated instructor can be as powerful—and misleading—a role model as a person from whom one has learned and benefited as a client. Classroom constructs can make human reality appear more schematic than it is. Moreover, the student role contains certain built-in support systems that are removed when a person goes out on the job. A trainee is not held fully accountable for decisions; a trainee is not penalized for mistakes; a trainee is not fired. Trainees can turn to their supervisors to set standards, define tasks, and correct errors. "I never realized," said a nurse at a nursing home, "that when I got out of nursing school those props would be removed. Now I was on my own—that was the harsh reality. Sometimes I wouldn't learn the right way to do something until after I had done it wrong."

Profile of a Novice Helper

Debbie W., a 21-year-old undergraduate student, is like many people who enter the helping professions even as they enter upon adult life. Debbie has the strengths of dedication and the limitations of inexperience. Her father was an alcoholic whose addiction eventually caused his death. Debbie thus experienced early the destructive effects of a serious psychosocial problem as well as the benefits of counseling. Between the ages of 11 and 18 she was seen by a family counselor, after which she went into individual therapy. To learn more about herself she began to take psychology courses, which in turn have led her to choose a career in the field. She has modeled herself after the woman therapist who she feels has helped her get beyond the traumas of her childhood.

Despite the fact that her family is poor, Debbie is going into counseling in the full knowledge that she will not earn as much money there as she might elsewhere. Being involved with people is more important to her than making money. Her primary goal at this time is to help the families of alcoholics. She is looking for credentials that will enable her to do so and that are obtainable in the shortest possible time.

Debbie is a serious person whose experiences have given her considerable self-awareness from an early age. She has the capacity to make a valuable contribution to other people's lives. But along with her genuine empathy and intelligence, there are some danger signals in her desire to finish her education quickly and in her choosing to help people who have the same problem she has had. Neither of these aims is necessarily wrong for her, but together they suggest that she is not sufficiently aware of the personal and professional complexities of a career in the helping professions. The appropriate interventions in her case are those that will make her more aware of the complexities before the fact, so that she can make realistic decisions concerning further education and employment. The nature of these interventions will be considered in Chapters 10 and 11.

EXPECTATIONS

When asked how they felt when they began their first job in the human services, people respond with words like "excited," "ecstatic," "overwhelmed," "thrilled," "elated," "lit up," "blessed," "chosen by God"—and also "anxious" and "terrified." Entering the helping professions is an intense emotional experience, with overtones of strong but diffuse anticipation. As a young person who plunged into the maelstrom of alcoholism treatment with a B.A. in sociology (and nothing more) put it, "I expected that I would be helping people, but I had no idea how!"

Expectations for Clients

A major component of the grandiose, mystical attitude that some of the above characterizations suggest is the idea that one's presence will make all the difference in the world to a client—that one's services will decisively alter the course of the client's life. This feeling has been aptly described as "narcissistic idealism." It is an exaggerated sense of one's importance in the scheme of things, a failure to realize the internal and external limits on one's effectiveness. Terms like "rescue complex" and "missionary zeal" have been used to capture the giddy feeling that all problems lie within one's purview and one's capacities for solution.

Expectations for Oneself

Closely related to the expectation of being a miracle worker is the less fully articulated expectation that the job will work a miracle *in one's own life.* Clearly, to succeed in changing the lives of others for the better would deeply enhance one's sense of potency as well as one's status and recognition in the world. The very hope of performing such miracles is perhaps a sign of unfulfilled yearnings that are being channeled into the job. A clinical psychologist who has negotiated several cycles of unrealistic expectations summed up the issue this way: "Any job is more exciting when it's new. The main thing is to realize that no job can be a total solution for your life."

The idea that, by performing certain services for people, one can work magical changes for them and for oneself is at the heart of all the unrealistic expectations that the novice helper brings to the job. These are the false hopes—for the client or for the counselor—whose eventual disappointment precipitates Burn-out.

Expectations of Simple Solutions

In the words of a social worker who has worked with state agencies in welfare, protective services, and family services, "people want a band-aid for their problems." This expectation is shared by enthusiastic workers who apply superficial remedies to eradicate long-standing, deeply ingrained patterns of self-destructive coping. A psychologist commented, "I used to think that people would change if you just spoke to them reasonably and forcefully. I had no idea how much resistance to change there is."

Expectations of Universal Success

The same psychologist, reflecting on her early days in practice, said, "There wasn't anyone I didn't think I could work with. It was a humiliation to me that I couldn't reach everyone." People just entering the field often do not realize that not every client will respond to a given counselor, not every counselor can work with a given client, and some clients (as well as some social problems) will not improve no matter who works with them.

Expectations of Immediate Success

Impatience is an occupational hazard in the helping professions—impatience like that expressed by the nursing administrator who exclaimed, "When I want to do something, I want to go out and do it tomorrow, if not yesterday. I want it *now.*" Time is a difficult, yet essential variable for the person who seeks to help others to come to terms with. It is a matter of recognizing that problems that have been building up for years cannot be solved in a day. As often as not, one does not have the opportunity to work with an individual or family over a long enough period to bring about (and observe) any meaningful change.

Expectations of Client Motivation

A teacher who had left the public school system traced her disillusionment in these words:

> What I learned most about in my first year or so as a teacher was myself. I came to realize that I had come into the classroom with four assumptions: first, that the students wanted to be there; second, that I had information to convey that was important to them; third, that they would be receptive to what I presented; fourth, that I knew more than they did. All of these assumptions were to some degree false.

It is natural, if ultimately disillusioning, to see one's clients as fitting neatly and cooperatively into one's own scheme of things, playing the roles that enable one to be of maximum assistance. On the basis of this assumption, many people extend themselves in helping others without stopping to question whether the people they are helping want to be helped. A woman with a master's degree in social work confessed, "It took me two years to realize that the motivation, the desire, was all mine, not theirs!"

Expectations of Control

The assumption that clients will play their assigned roles slips easily into the expectation that one can maneuver them into those roles. The school psychologist who hopes to "socialize children into behavior that creates less anxiety for them" may not be aware of all the ways in which children simultaneously socialize their teachers. Positions that carry a great deal of apparent formal authority, such as those of the schoolteacher and workshop group leader, create an aura of power that dissipates amid the complexities of day-to-day functioning.

Expectations of Appreciation

People who do things for others want to be appreciated by the people they are helping. In particular, those who model themselves after a revered teacher or therapist may unconsciously wish to be loved and respected as much as they love and respect the individual who inspired them to go into the field —which is a tall order. Appreciation requires that clients acknowledge the services that are performed and accept them as beneficial, and this is something many clients do not sit still long enough to do.

Expectations of Direct Contact with Clients

When Debbie W., the young student whose expectations have not yet been tempered by experience, was given the 12-point planning board exercise described in Chapter 1, she was asked to rank the items on the basis of what she anticipated it would be like to have a job in the human services. Debbie gave high rankings to items such as "not appreciated by clients," "not appreciated by supervisor," and "not sufficiently trained for the job." She gave the lowest ranking to "paper work." People who have had some experience in the field generally rank "paper work" considerably higher. For Debbie, however, issues involving direct client services and client relations were more salient than organizational and bureaucratic issues.

Debbie's choices reflect the outlook of a person for whom the confrontation with reality is still in the future. Few people go into the human services in order to be bureaucrats; it is the expectation of being able to work directly with people that attracts them. "I went into nursing because I wanted my work to be of immediate practical benefit to people—I wanted to be right there on the front lines and see the results of my efforts." This statement typifies the spirit of the helper. But the person who spoke these words, like others in her field and related fields, faces a constant struggle to keep this sense of directness and immediacy from being lost in the administrative requirements of the job, let alone those of career advancement.

Expectations of Specific, Concrete Tasks

The novice helper, although very sure that he or she wants to work directly with people, is often a lot less sure about just what he or she is going to be doing for them. Furthermore, the person who thinks he or she does know what the actual day-to-day work will entail is often wrong. A social worker with a master's degree recalled that, when she began training, "I thought being a social worker meant delivering Thanksgiving baskets to needy families." This image of concrete services represents a common misconception about social work. People who start out expecting to deliver Thanksgiving baskets usually will need to adjust to actual responsibilities that are considerably more subtle and diffuse.

Expectations of a Rewarding Work Environment

The first taste of work in the helping professions often is a stimulating one. The protective environment of school and the heady atmosphere of groups or workshops are good for building enthusiasm, but they do not give a person a very good idea of what lies ahead. In the course of a professional or paraprofessional career one must learn to work in environments—some of them isolated and lonely, some tense with divided responsibility—that are not so immediately nurturant.

Expectations of Further Training

People expect to learn on the job. In human services jobs there is a good deal of learning, much of it of the unplanned, unanticipated sort described here, i.e., an exposure to the various ways in which reality fails to meet expectations. The kind of on-the-job training that people expect—and are led to expect—is more formal in nature. This expectation, too, is as often disappointed as met. Many individuals accept unglamorous paraprofessional jobs in the hope that these will serve as an entry point for further work and higher-level qualification in the field; sometimes this hope turns out to be a mere promise. A psychiatric technician who aspired to be a clinical psychologist grumbled, "I was told I would get real training, not a once-a-week formality."

Expectations of Status

Training programs tend to glorify the future prospects of trainees, thus feeding the aspirations to status that many already have. "Everybody in the program wanted to be a private psychotherapist," a psychiatric social worker remarked of her fellow students, "but how many actually could?" When people's expectations are not realistically channeled, when there are too few positions available to employ more than a fraction of the people who expect to attain such positions, disillusionment is inevitable.

THE CYCLE OF EXPECTATIONS

The belief in magic dies hard. Although one sobering experience may innoculate a person against extravagant expectations in the future, it just as often does not. Several such experiences will tend to have a greater effect, but by then the person may have gone through the entire Burn-out cycle several times. In one sense it is good that human beings are so resilient emotionally, for this capacity enables them to recapture their enthusiasm, and with it their energy and effectiveness in another job or work setting. But it also leaves them open to repeated disillusionment.

How is it that one can persist in unrealistic hopes even when these are ostensibly disconfirmed? One does so by concluding not that the magical solution has failed, but that one has not yet found the right formula. The original hope of speedy, consistent, visible cures is still held out, with the proviso that a vital "missing ingredient" for achieving those cures has yet to be obtained. Take the case of Paula G., a middle-aged woman who came to alcoholism counseling with a strong Alcoholics Anonymous background but no further professional training. At first she thought that the A.A. approach was right for everyone, but to her discouragement she quickly learned otherwise. As the case load piled up, straining her skills and energies to the limit, Paula realized that she needed further training, so she enrolled in a program in family counseling. This was a constructive step for her, but she was still too inexperienced to place it in proper perspective. Instead, she ascribed the kind of potency to it that she previously associated with A.A. "Once I learn family counseling," one could almost hear her say, "I'll get that backlog of cases moving again."

For Paula, family counseling was the "missing ingredient" that would give her the "answer," the magic. For Debbie W., the missing ingredient was education. In the first flush of excitement over what she was learning in her psychology classes, she began to envision herself saving the world on the strength of her book-learning. An experienced counselor or trainer could have told Paula or Debbie that one is never sufficiently educated, never sufficiently trained to deal with everything one will face in practice. Each new skill acquired only makes a person more aware of the need for additional skills. All of those skills together can give a person as many perspectives as possible from which to face problems that remain various, complex, and baffling.

The quest for the elusive missing ingredient is expressed in the "wait till . . ." or "now that . . ." phenomenon. "Wait till I get my next set of credentials; then things will be different." "Now that I know where it's *really* at . . ." "Once I get to be an administrator," says the junior high school guidance counselor, "I'll be able to assign myself direct contact with students instead of all this paper work I'm tied down with now. I look forward to the new challenges and new opportunities that lie ahead." This is the voice of inexperience, the voice of anticipatory enthusiasm.

As if in reply to such sunny expectations, one who has been a top administrator—the director of a far-flung university social service program—tells what some of those new challenges and opportunities might turn out to be like:

> When I began the program I was a dilettante. Never having been trained as an administrator, I had no systematic approach—just some flashy ideas of social usefulness. Once I realized that we couldn't be everything to everybody, I settled down and devel-

oped a plan. We selected the programs we could support on a sustained basis, instead of doing a lot of things hit-or-miss. Did things get better now that I knew what I was doing? No—that was when my greatest frustrations occurred. As the concept and the theoretical framework took shape, I began to get ambitious. We began to think of ourselves as the wave of the future, only we were a bit too far in the future for those who made up the university budget. That took a lot out of me—to have good ideas, to be pragmatic, to be responsible, and still to be stopped from doing everything I wanted to do.

Here, knowledge and realism about the task at hand turned out to be a prelude to frustration. It is a clear illustration of the cycle of enthusiastic expectation, where one disillusionment sets a person up for the next.

A Portrait of the Enthusiast

Enthusiasm comes not only from high initial motivation, but from early successes and satisfactions on the job. The new counselor or social worker, needing a certain amount of structure and supervision, tends to be put to work in environments that are safer and more rewarding than those that he or she will face later. One such milieu is the workshop or therapy group. Here, in a contagion of positive enthusiasm, the energy of the novice is reinforced by that of peers, supervisors, and clients, and some easy successes result.

Another example is the orientation where new workers are given textbook responses to use in idealized situations. These briefings, although technically and clinically sound, may have little or no bearing on the problems that will occur in day-to-day practice. For instance, a protective services caseworker is told what to say in order to gain entry to a house where child abuse is suspected. In practice, this standard approach will work only in a small proportion of cases. Only with experience will the worker be able to size up the situation and come up with the appropriate intervention.

Ironically, the least experienced, lowest-status person (e.g., the front-line crisis counselor, the ward nurse) often has the most direct contact with clients, which in turn makes possible the satisfaction of directly observing the results of one's efforts. True, there are not only successes, but the person who is primed to look for success finds ample positive reinforcement. At this stage, the anticipatory "high" that the newcomer is riding is continually renewed. The reinforcement, however, is largely internal. It consists of the thrill of actually doing the job for the first time, together with a certain amount of positive feedback that one pays attention to precisely because it matches one's expectations.

Later, when one has moved out into tougher, more demanding environments—and exhausted one's capacity for self-reinforcement as well—one tends to look back upon these halcyon days with a certain wistful nostalgia. "Why can't things be like the old days," one asks, "when all I did was run from one workshop to another?" Or as a counselor in one of the military services put it:

> When I had my first job supervising the corrections center on base, I had people up and down the echelons of command interested in me and in what I was doing. I needed training and guidance, and my country gave it to me. It was all new to me, and it was magnificent. I wish I had never been transferred out of there. Somehow since then it's never been the same.

Unlimited Commitment

Enthusiasm takes the form of an overinvestment of oneself in the job. It is remarkable how nearly universal this phenomenon is. In this regard no distinction can be made between the drug counselor directly out of Daytop Village and the professionally trained psychologist or social worker; it is the same at all levels of education and status. Almost everyone reports having worked 12 to 16 hours a day, six or seven days a week at the outset. Allusions to "missionary zeal" and unsparing self-sacrifice are common. No effort is withheld that might save a soul, or at least benefit a client. As one counselor recalls, "I'd go fifteen miles to fix a broken shoelace. I'd throw my wife out of bed to answer the beeper."

Typically, the new (and not so new) social servant will bring work home—if not the work itself, then the concerns of the work day. A man who at the age of 30 had been working in the prison system for five years conceded, "In a way I still bring things home with me, as much as I try not to. I have to put a lot of energy into trying not to do that." As a consequence of this overcommitment to work, there is not much energy left over for one's personal life—to the extent that one has a personal life. Family relationships suffer, and a single person's social life may become nonexistent. But these effects are hardly noticed when one's head is filled with the image of cheering crowds.

In the stage of enthusiasm, it is commonly felt that the job is one's whole life, and that all of one's gratifications are coming from the job. This unbalanced existence (or "small world," to use William Glasser's term) comes about by a kind of vicious cycle. On the one hand, one's inflated conception of the job tends to obliterate personal needs and concerns, at least temporarily. But the reverse may also be true—i.e., one's glorification of work may itself arise from deficiencies in one's personal life.

The latter is most clearly observable in alcoholism and addiction counselors who, as recovering addicts, may literally have had no constructive life before taking the job. As one such state employee put it, "At first all that mattered was that I was somebody in the straight world. My new life was here." Money and working hours do not matter to the person who derives so much status from the job. This attitude is, however, by no means limited to the ex-substance abuser or prison inmate; no one is immune to it, even the psychiatric resident who has a husband or wife waiting at home every day. Furthermore, the cycle of overcommitment is self-fulfilling, for the longer one neglects one's personal life, the more it deteriorates. One is thus left in a highly vulnerable position when the job ceases to furnish the rewards it once did.

Enthusiasm of this sort has both positive and negative effects on client services. Enthusiasm engenders effort as well as involvement, and as Lee Silverstein has made very clear in *Consider the Alternative,*[1] involvement is probably the major factor in successful counseling. At least at the start, then, enthusiasm sets in motion a positive feedback cycle: enthusiasm is contagious; effort pays off; and successful results inspire continued enthusiasm. The danger of enthusiasm, by the testimony of those who have gone through it, comes from an "arrogant" or "grandiose" view of oneself that covers up a superficial and inadequate knowledge of what one is doing. This is what one social worker has called "the arrogance of ignorance." A crisis group leader remarked, "I was immediately given responsibility for making decisions, and I made some wrong decisions, like blaming the victim. Only later did I realize that I didn't yet know what therapy was." As we shall see, there is also the hazard of overidentification. The counselor whose own needs are overly invested in the job will inappropriately subject clients to the pressure to conform to expectations.

The quintessential enthusiast is the "born again" addict or alcoholic who begins life in the straight world as a front-line counselor in the addictions field. In the case of Roger F., who later described himself as having been "just one step ahead of the addicts I was counseling," we have a vivid self-portrait of the self-important novice who appears, albeit in more subtle guises, throughout the helping professions:

> At the beginning my background was my repertoire. I thought I had it all knocked because I came from Daytop. The professionals who supervised me apparently thought so, too. They thought the words "relate," "cop-out," and "where you're coming from" were a kind of magic that I could work on a group. Actually, I didn't know what I was doing, and I didn't know that

I didn't know. I picked up some cliches, confronted people without any sense of proper timing, and thought that was counseling. But what I lacked in knowledge and technique, I made up for in enthusiasm. Since I really believed in what I was doing, the addicts I worked with believed in me, too. I did some of my best work during this period.

My job was my life. I identified with it totally. The groups I ran were *my* groups. I arranged the chairs in a circle before the group, and I swept up afterward. God help anyone who dropped an ash on my floor. On Saturdays I was all over the city hunting up my clients: "Did you get a job yet? Did you register for school? Did you write to your mother?" I quivered with pride in what I was doing. Nothing else mattered. Work hours were not an issue. My subsistence-level pay was not an issue. Nor was my social life or my sex life. All my strokes came from the job.

OVERIDENTIFICATION

Overidentification with clients is a major link in the chain that stretches from enthusiasm to Burn-out, both because it leads the helper to act in ways that are detrimental to clients and because it makes the helper's emotional well-being depend on clients living up to unrealistic expectations. Overidentification stems from an excess of energy and dedication, a lack of knowledge and experience in the field, and a confusion of one's own needs with those of clients. It manifests itself as a lack of clarity in role definitions between client and helper. What are the limits of involvement? How far does a counselor's commitment extend? When do professional obligations turn into social and personal obligations? Overidentification leads to unlimited commitment and a blurring of the boundaries both between the client's life and the counselor's and between the counselor's working life and personal life. It leads well-meaning professionals and paraprofessionals to make themselves available, say, to receive phone calls at home at all hours of the night—a degree of accessibility that can have damaging effects on one's own life. Overidentification takes different forms at different levels of professional training and involvement. The following cases illustrate how overidentification occurs and how it affects clients and helpers in the various strata of the profession.

The Paraprofessional Counselor

Paula G., who is expanding upon her background in alcoholism by taking additional training in family counseling, describes a case which showed her how easy it was for her to overidentify in both areas:

> I was seeing a 50-year-old woman who came in originally because her husband was beating her, but who also had a drinking problem, which she came to acknowledge in the course of her work with me. Together we did succeed in getting her sober and getting her into A.A. But when it came to her marital problem, I think I was too receptive to her side of the story because it reminded me of my own story. I wanted to believe that her husband was to blame for her drinking because that's what I wanted to believe about my drinking. When I finally got around to having her husband come in with her, I found that the dynamics were completely different from what she had led me to believe. The "black sheep" was really quite considerate, and he had troubles of his own with her. I saw that I had acted less as a therapist than as a friend to this woman, and that was not what I was being paid to be.

Paula lacked the knowledge and skill to deal with countertransference. Her overidentification left her vulnerable to manipulation—not only by this client and others, but by staff members whose reaction to her extraordinary empathy with clients was, "Good old Paula—we'll dump these people on her." It is common for counselors who think of their clients as fellow addicts to feel that they have "lost a friend" when a client goes back to drinking or the street life. This degree of involvement works very well in A.A., but it can compromise a professional therapeutic relationship.

The B.A.-level Idealist

The person who comes to social work straight from college courses in sociology, anthropology, or psychology is nearly as vulnerable to overidentification and emotional impositions by clients as the recovering addict. Catherine Y., who in her early 20s worked at a counseling center for female adolescent delinquents, describes what for her was a source of vulnerability as well as sensitivity:

> Although I never got in trouble with the law, I had been regarded as something of a behavior problem myself, so I really identified with those girls. They had weight problems; so did I. They had problems with boyfriends; so did I. Working in that live-in facility I never did get to see my boyfriend enough, so it was easy to empathize. One thing that closeness did was to win me the confidence and trust of the girls. They accepted me as a friend. But by being a friend to them I probably gave away too much. I sat and ate with them instead of probing the dynamics of their weight problems. And when one of them would act out or go back to her old behavior, I'd get very upset. I would go up to my room and cry. I liked those girls and had invested so much time in them that I just didn't understand why they didn't want to do something for themselves. I couldn't stand to see them throw it all away. Since then I've developed a more professional attitude. I know enough not to react personally to what my clients do, and I focus on meeting the client's needs, not my own. But I still think it's valid, if I'm going to be honest in my work, to apply to myself what I say to the people I'm helping, and to ask myself if I have any of the same problems they do.

Catherine's tendency to personalize, her sense of a bond between herself and her clients, is both her strength and her weakness. It has enabled her to share with the people she counsels and to inspire them to identify reciprocally with her. It also has made her unnecessarily fragile in facing the stresses of her work, but her honesty about herself has made it possible for her to recognize and compensate for that problem.

The Professionally Trained Social Worker

A person with a graduate degree (including field experience) in social work—one who has learned through supervised training a set of attitudes and techniques for dealing with people professionally—is unlikely to burst into tears when a client misbehaves or "backslides." But no amount of training can protect a person from overidentification altogether. Sandra K., who has an M.S.W. and works in family services, speaks of overidentification in its subtler forms:

> When I went into counseling I was already raising adolescent children, and I think I have always modeled my role as a counselor after my role as a mother. At first I did things for clients that they should have done for themselves, such as making contacts to arrange job interviews. In doing so I laid expectations on the client and left myself open for frustration when the client didn't follow through. When my field supervisor pointed out that I was relating to clients in a mothering way, I tried to detach myself, probably to the detriment of my work. I lost something positive that way. What I needed to do was to create a nurturant role for the *client,* but not to get emotionally involved in that role myself. This, I feel, has become my great strength as a counselor —to give people the nurturance, the mothering, that they have lacked and that they need.

The Clinical Psychologist or Psychiatrist

The intimacy and intensity of the psychotherapeutic relationship create special problems of countertransference. Marilyn P., a clinical psychologist in private practice, has experienced her share of these and has developed guidelines which (like Sandra's) are useful for coping with them.

> In training I had all the usual reactions to people who resisted or failed to respond to treatment. I got angry and blamed them, but underneath I felt inadequate—and with good reason. My

supervisor taught me to recognize the limits on what I could do for people and to let people go if I couldn't help them. I believe that I'm still learning to be realistic about this, and that being realistic about myself helps me be realistic about others.

One problem that I still face is that of countertransference with male clients. I know now that it's when I'm unhappy, when I'm frustrated in my personal life, that I'm susceptible to the impulse to use clients for sexual and ego-gratification. Many therapists, male and female, deny any feeling of attraction to their clients. Instead, it comes out in headaches, anger, or a kind of flirtation where they tease themselves as well as the client. My approach is to accept those feelings and get beyond them by assuming certain limits on my behavior. I say to myself, "I'd like to do this if it were possible, but it's not, so I won't expend any energy on it." In other words, instead of letting the tension build up I try to diffuse it.

Avoiding Overidentification

Everyone in the helping professions must frequently make delicate discriminations between appropriate therapeutic involvement with a client and overinvolvement. It is difficult, but necessary, to decide how much is too much. A social services case worker in a state agency describes some of the things she used to do with and for clients that she no longer does:

> I would get invited to weddings, bar mitzvahs, and so forth, and for a while I used to go to these affairs. That was when I was still trying to be a friend and confidant to the people I was working with instead of offering them avenues for change. Now I politely decline all such invitations. My having social relationships with clients wasn't doing them any good; it was more for my own sake.

Experienced counselors find it helpful to set up general criteria to call upon when situations of this sort come up. These are the guidelines that one such counselor maintains for himself and teaches to his students:

> If establishing a relationship with a client means telling him what teams I root for, what movies I like, what food I enjoy, I'll tell

him. My sex life, how much money I make—these are no one's business. If establishing a relationship means sending someone a birthday card or Christmas card, if it means calling someone from time to time or going out for coffee, that's fine. But not if it means lending someone money or going to bed with her.

When I work for an agency, my qualifications are a matter to be settled between me and my employer. They are not subject to discussion with clients. I am not obligated to justify myself to clients by telling them what degrees I have, how long I have worked in the field, or whether or not I have been an addict. Self-disclosure is a tool of the trade that I employ at my own discretion, not when I am pressured to do so. I speak about my background or my feelings only when my doing so will benefit the client or student. I do not do so to create a "high" for myself or for anyone else.

THE PRICE OF REALISM

If a person is to succeed—or just survive—in the human services field, overidentification must give way to a degree of detachment. A woman who, like Catherine Y., used to "bury my head in my hands and cry" when faced with a recalcitrant client reported that in similar situations now she "breaks things off. If someone doesn't want to be helped, I just turn off and send him back where he came from." Once enthusiastic, this woman is close to apathy. The large question that this book addresses is how to keep the detachment that is necessary for working with people from souring into apathy.

A young administrator in a government-funded social service program came to her first job with expectations which (in contrast to many that we have seen) were remarkable for their realism:

> As an affirmative action officer you get a title, a good salary, and access to the director. Then nothing happens. You make recommendations that the director does not implement. It took me a week to realize that. But then, I didn't go in with any illusions.

This woman, a humane and effective worker, had so few illusions about social work that she had no desire to be a social worker in the first place. She felt that she could do more for people as a government planner. The dilemma facing those who *are* dedicated to human services is to be realistic enough to cope with discouraging conditions without thereby suffering a total loss of idealism and concern. This is also the lesson that needs to be conveyed to students and trainees. It is the place where intervention is most crucial, especially when we reflect that an initial *lack* of realism is what leaves one most vulnerable to eventual disillusionment.

Chapter 4

THE SMALL WORLD OF STAGNATION

People sometimes wonder why stagnation precedes frustration in the four stages of Burn-out. "A person gets frustrated," they say, "and then becomes stagnated." In our scheme, however, "apathy" is the term used to represent the chronic loss of concern that follows repeated frustrations. *Stagnation* refers to something different—namely, the process of becoming stalled after an initial burst of enthusiasm. It is the loss of the momentum of hope and desire that brings a person into the helping field.

Obviously, no sharp line can be drawn between stagnation and frustration, or between any two of the four stages of Burn-out. The progression through the four stages is not something that can be traced in precise chronological sequence in any given case. (Indeed, depending on one's mood and the aspect of the job one is occupied with, one can have feelings of enthusiasm, stagnation, frustration, and apathy—all on the very same day!) But it does give us a sense of the overall pattern of Burn-out.

Some of the frustrations that we will discuss in Chapters

6 through 8 can, of course, begin to occur before or during the stage of stagnation. Those beginnings of frustration are part of what brings about stagnation, for they represent the disconfirmation of great expectations. When one is engaged in superhuman exploits, it does not matter so much that one is living a less than human life. When one's accomplishments are reduced to human scale, then minor annoyances such as low pay and long hours begin to be noticed. The frustrations that occur at this point are not enough to make one question doing the job, but they are enough to make one question doing nothing but the job.

That is stagnation: one is still doing the job, but the job can no longer make up for the fact that one's personal needs are not being met—the need to earn a decent living, to be respected on and off the job, to have satisfying family and social relationships and some leisure time in which to enjoy them. If those needs remain unmet, one will not be able to keep on doing the job for very long.

Stagnation is the obverse of enthusiasm. It is a "revolution of unfulfilled expectations." To find the causes of stagnation, all we have to do is turn back to the previous chapter and review the list of common expectations with which people enter the human services field. To summarize briefly (and in a way that is not meant to be applied literally to any individual case), one who is just starting out in the field expects to be able to work directly with clients—but not with so many clients that one will not have sufficient time for each. Because one's own purpose is to help people one does not consider that this may not be the purpose of either the clients or the agency, both of which may be more interested in helping *themselves* in whatever way they see fit. Instead, one assumes that clients want to be helped and that the helping agency exists to serve that end. One believes that good intentions plus whatever training one has had (professional, academic, "street savvy," or none at all) will enable one to be of service to a reasonable number of people in a reasonably short time, and that the results of one's efforts will be apparent to oneself and others. For these successes, one expects to be rewarded by supervisors and appreciated by clients.

The fate of such expectations is universal; it cuts through all gradations of education and status. True, in discussing stagnation we will be emphasizing the personal deprivations—of income, of recognition, of influence, of autonomy—that hit hardest at the paraprofessional, the college graduate without professional training, the working professional without a graduate degree. But we should not for a moment lose sight of the fact that everyone up and down the ladder finds doubts settling in after a period of time on the job. The psychologist or psychiatrist who expects every clinical hour to give fresh evidence of her power to change people, the program administrator who expects the board of directors to applaud whenever he comes up with a new way of spending money to help the community —they are no strangers to stagnation.

ELUSIVE RESULTS

Stagnation often begins with the discovery that it is not as easy as anticipated to see, let alone assess, the results of one's labors. This tends to be a chronic rather than an acute frustration, in that its disillusioning effects are not felt all at once. Initially it is experienced not as a source of active discontent, but as a kind of puzzlement that leaves one wondering why the job is not quite what it was cracked up to be.

Some of the clearest insights into the question of the measurability of results have been given by counselors in the military services. Many of these men are not career counselors. Typically, they began their military careers in a technical field and then switched to the "people field" after having themselves gone through some personal trauma (often alcoholism). Quite commonly they will remark that their present work "feels different" from what they used to do. Why? The answer will sound something like this:

When I worked on a nuclear submarine, there was no question about whether or not I had done my job. "Is it ready?" the boss would say. And it had to *be* ready—all done to specification by the designated time. But what do I have to go on now? I have to be content when once in a while someone whom I've helped waves to me from across the street.

How can I feel that I'm accomplishing anything when I see my whole counseling staff turn over in two or three years? Sometimes I think it would be easier just to "turn over" myself and go back to "normal duty." But I stay in the field because this duty gives my life meaning. Normal duty didn't do that for me; if it had, I wouldn't have been drinking.

This is the struggle—to find meaning for oneself in an activity whose meaning is always just out of reach.

People who go into counseling from civilian careers in business or industry (whether or not as a result of alcoholism) face the same adjustment. A woman who made this transition commented, "In business there's always a bottom line, a point where you have to produce. In counseling it's easier to duck responsibility by passing it off to the client, or to any of a number of other people or agencies. There's always somebody to blame, and as a result no standards are maintained." Yet, like the military counselor, she could see the other side of the story as well: "A corporation can easily replace any individual. In my work with individuals and families the person-to-person connection makes me as an individual uniquely valuable. It's one human being to another."

Many people confront this issue without consciously identifying it. A trained scientist who decided that she did not want to do academic research became the director of an outreach program for disadvantaged youths. In the chaotic atmosphere of what she described as "impossible problems," she searched for a way to verify the progress she was making. Finally she said, "Our contribution is in being catalysts. We start projects that will develop their own momentum and go on without us." With these words, spoken in the language of a physicist, she sought to justify what she was doing in terms of the standards she was trained to meet.

She also was pointing out a major reason why it is so hard to measure success in the helping professions—namely, the fact that the helpers often do not have the opportunity to keep track of their clients long enough to see how much they have benefited. This is most clearly the case in an acute care situation such as a crisis-line referral service, where only short-term goals are feasible and where the helper does not spend enough time with the client to develop a strong identification. The crisis-line worker does, of course, have the option of imagining that the clients who pass by in front of the desk will all show great improvement elsewhere: more concrete verification is hard to come by.

The opposite kind of situation—the one where the helper does get to see the clients over a long period of time precisely because they do *not* show improvement—has problems of its own. Here the subtle benefits of the helper's ministrations may be much less visible than the stark reality that one cannot change nature. Seeing the same patients year after year on a chronic care ward of a hospital or mental institution can be demoralizing for a nurse whose childhood aspiration was "to help people get well." Placed in such a setting, one may well exclaim, "What am I really doing?" Or, as a nurse with experience on both medical and psychiatric units put it,

> In life-or-death situations my first reaction is to ask, "What did I do wrong?" Somehow every life depends on my knowledge and my actions; I forget that everybody dies sooner or later. In mental health, too, there is a grinding pressure that never quite lets up. Every now and then I could use a complete cure, but in mental health there rarely is one.

According to a psychologist who practices and teaches at a university mental health clinic, "Clinical work is by its very nature intangible. You can't expect to get grades or commendations. You have to learn to be satisfied with your experience and the client's." The same is true in any helping situation—acute or chronic, inpatient or outpatient, professional or paraprofessional. Its importance for stagnation lies in the fact that when one cannot be sure what one is accomplishing, one is all the more likely to look to the immediate environment—i.e., one's co-workers—for help in defining the value of one's efforts. A number of well-known experiments in social psychology[1] have shown that people given the task of characterizing visual stimuli (e.g., which of two lines on a wall poster is longer, where a point of light is located in a dark room) are very susceptible to the influence of others even when the identifying features of the stimuli are clear-cut, let alone when they are vague. In the helping professions, where results are not at all clear-cut, people find it only natural to look to those around them for an answer to the question, "What am I doing, anyway?" Given the climate of the typical helping agency, the answer they get from more experienced staff members tends to have strong negative overtones.

CONTAGION OF ATTITUDES

One of the marks of enthusiasm is the tendency to allow the job to become one's whole world. At that point, of course, it looks like a very large world. When the job still promises to be a vast field for accomplishment, one does not think that one is limiting oneself by associating primarily with one's co-workers. But in so doing one is drawing boundaries around oneself, defining oneself by what may be the parochial outlook of a few people with whom one works every day. Attitudes, like germs, spread rapidly in a stuffy atmosphere.

Socializing with the Staff

Every day at 5 P.M. when the day shift on the inpatient psychiatric ward at Center City Hospital goes off duty, the nurses and technicians adjourn to a bar across the street. There, in the dim light and tobacco-heavy air, they continue treating the patients they have been seeing all day. No longer are they wrestling with patients who require physical restraint, but they are still wrestling with treatment decisions—reliving them, debating them, revising them in preparation for the next day.

Is this dedication or overdedication? Leaving aside for the moment its effects on the personal lives of ward personnel, we can see that it is a way of transmitting the attitudes of the group to the individual worker, particularly the worker who has just come on board. In these informal meetings as well as in the course of the day's work, staff members let each other know what must be done for the good of the patients (and for the good of the staff). They also let each other know what need *not* be done, and what there is no point even in attempting to do. Along with this information an attitude or set of attitudes is conveyed. And when people regularly find it necessary to gravitate en masse to a bar to rehash the day's work, that attitude is likely to be one of being burdened, weighed down, of not being able to get out from under the demands and discouragements of the job.

Gatherings like these, on and off the job, take different forms in different settings. The staff of one psychiatric clinic periodically arranges office parties "to clear the air whenever the tension gets thick." According to one of the technicians, "sometimes it works, and sometimes people just sit there." Such meetings, intended as a forum for airing grievances, may just as often reinforce the participants' sense of having something to be aggrieved about. New staff members learn that one way to deal with frustrations and difficulties is to blame them on clients, supervisors, or the institution. Is there a school, for example, that does not have daily or weekly "bitching sessions" in the faculty lounge? Here is one teacher's account of what goes on there:

When teachers get together in the teachers' room they mainly talk about the kids. Sometimes they do it to get confirmation of how they feel about a student. They want somebody to say, "Man, that kid really *is* rotten." Sometimes they do it to get real feedback about what's going on with a student and how he or she can best be handled. And sometimes they do it just to talk away their anxieties.

I believe that this process is inevitable and necessary. But whether it is constructive depends on what you do with it. If you get the bitching against students and administration out of your system, if you leave it there in the room, fine. What isn't good is if you carry it back into the classroom.

If this informal communication process is so highly developed among teachers, who go home to their families each afternoon, it is even stronger in a residential facility such as a drug or alcohol rehabilitation center where the counselors live with the patients. But whatever the setting, the significance of the process is the same: when people "socialize" in the conventional sense of the word, they are "socialized" in the sense in which the word is used by anthropologists and sociologists.

Co-optation by Veteran Staff Members

What are the values into which new personnel are socialized? Sometimes they are constructive ones. In one psychiatric treatment facility where the attending physicians are almost all first-year residents in training, much of the responsibility for patient care falls to the nursing staff, which includes mental health workers who lack prior training in the field. These individuals would not survive on the job, let alone make a contribution, without some form of peer supervision. And this, as the senior member of the staff explains, is just what they get:

You're there for a week learning the patients' names, and then you're asked, "Can you do it?" That's the formal training. The rest of the training consists of doing it the best you can with support and also pressure from the people who have been doing it a little longer than you—long enough to know that they need your help.

This is one place where dedicated people are admired, and new people are told, "Don't get discouraged." That does not mean that there is no Burn-out here. For here, and elsewhere, new people are given a contrary message as well.

When Randy W., a medical aide in a military hospital, reported to the nurses' station with his shoes shined and his white uniform neatly pressed for his first day on duty, the wardmaster (chief medical technician) told him to take the vital signs of all the patients on the ward. Instantly Randy propelled himself down the hall with giant steps, his arms chopping at the air like wings. He seemed to feel that he should be busily in motion every second that he was being paid (at little more than the minimum wage). The wardmaster looked up with surprise. "Whoa!" he said. "Take it easy. Save your energy for when you really need it. You won't make it through one eight-hour shift that way. And if you do get through the first day, you won't get through the first week!"

This was the voice of experience speaking—the voice of realism and, in this case, good sense. But the voice of experience does not stop there. Very often the wardmaster's advice to Randy is generalized into more subtle and wider-ranging cautionary messages to the enthusiastic newcomer. The warning, "You'll burn yourself out that way," does not only apply to an inexperienced medical assistant squandering his day-to-day physical energy. It can be—and is—used to discourage people from trying "too hard" to help clients, from being too innovative, from trying to revitalize a stagnant organization. As a counselor in the prison system reports,

Each new trainee is watched closely by the old-line staff. "Here comes another one," they say to themselves. "How far is he going to go? Wait till he learns. Wait till the inmates start running games on him. Wait till he gets worn down by the daily grind while the bureaucracy builds up walls for him to bang his head against."

They say these things about the new person and *to* him as well. They're jealous of him—jealous of his energy, his idealism, his willingness to work—all the qualities they once had. They're jealous of the opportunities he may have if their dire predictions don't come true. Every new person is a threat to them, and so they respond with a threat in the form of friendly advice, friendly warnings that he'd better not violate the norms of the institution.

The biggest threat is the person with new ideas about how to run the place, ideas that may "shake things up," disrupt established patterns, threaten secure positions, maybe even make some people work a little harder. And so from Randy rushing down the hall we go all the way up to the newly hired administrator facing a staff that only wants to be reassured that no real innovations will be attempted.

A poignant account of the demoralization brought about in part by what is felt as peer pressure comes from a teacher who left the public school system after having an emotional collapse:

> The feedback I got for my efforts from other teachers was largely negative. My enthusiasm was an affront to their complacency. A department head with 21 years' experience used to brag that she didn't bother to keep up with the literature in her field anymore —hadn't read a book in ages. She would turn to me in the teachers' room or at a social gathering and say, "Why don't you just cool it? You'll do a lot better if you just realize that nobody cares anyway. You're always trying to rock the boat." That wasn't even true. I am basically conservative and rather orderly in my teaching methods. I just wanted to stimulate the students, that's all.
>
> Where were my allies, meanwhile? One or two other teachers who felt the way I did have left the system, too. One of them

—still a young man, and a person I had valued greatly as a colleague—died of a heart attack a year or so later.

In Chapter 6 we will see how bureaucratic pressure—i.e., the actual political constraints of the system—reinforces this peer pressure.

As the inexperienced worker is socialized into a defeatist —or defeated—attitude by fellow staff members, enthusiasm turns to stagnation. And the contagion spreads in all directions. When the individuals working in an organization stagnate, the organization stagnates. When the organization stagnates, it does not take long for the "fresh new blood" it hires to go sour. And stagnant workers in a stagnant agency are not about to get clients moving in new directions.

The overwhelming power of the process is shown by the energy it takes to oppose it. A middle manager in a social services program who confessed that "much of my job is preventing Burn-out among the staff" described the drain this placed on her energies when she said, "I have to keep myself up to keep them from being down." Her aim was to transmit positive attitudes to her staff by a kind of reverse contagion— and that in itself was a full-time job.

Back at the psychiatric ward where informal daily staff meetings take place after work at the bar across the street, resistance to the contagion of Burn-out has come from a surprising source—new staff members themselves, one of whom told a senior colleague, "We don't want to hear about your problems. If we can't lean on you, what do we have to keep us going?"

Effects on Personal and Family Life

The recovering alcoholic who faces a daily procession of fellow sufferers without ever having heard the word "triage" may not look very much like the director of a university clinical psychology program who has to "make an effort" to keep from sneaking back into the office on evenings and weekends. Both, however, are living in what William Glasser (in *Positive Addiction*[2]) calls a "small world," a world where one's basic satisfactions in life come from one source. Their lives centered in their work, both may complain of a "lack of energy" for other pursuits. Long hours on the job, whether the result of enthusiasm or necessity or (as is most often the case) both, tend to tie a person down within the confines of the job. Amid the overload of clients that the helper voluntarily or involuntarily takes on, personal needs are swept aside. The person with a well-established family or social life may see it jeopardized. The person who is not so well connected is likely to remain isolated.

The effects on family life become apparent when a dedicated welfare caseworker finds that she has given herself so completely to her clients during the day that she does not have quite enough patience for her husband and children in the evening. A professionally trained social worker confesses rather poignantly:

> The time taken away from my family life has been an immeasurable loss to me. As a mother I can't reclaim those years when my children were young and when I could not be with them as much as I wanted to. As a single parent I have also had trouble balancing my social life against my family life and balancing both against my work. I have seen people end up friendless after working 14 hours a day for several years to get a master's or doctor's degree. For me it has been a matter of constantly questioning how dedicated I am to my goal as against other values in my life. This conflict has no resolution; I live with it from week to week like a television serial.

Although the last sentence of this passage sounds grim, it expresses a mature facing of reality. By being so well aware of the persistent conflict between the claims of work and motherhood, this woman has avoided the kind of sharp imbalance in her life that might, for example, have caused her to try to be too much a mother to her clients.

The effects of overcommitment to work on marriage include a kind of contagion where not only the individual's life but the couple's is swept up into the demands of the job. The wife of a psychiatric nurse describes her running battle to preserve some open space in her life for other concerns:

> When Jeff comes home from work, all he wants to talk about is the job. He mumbles about his patients in his sleep. It's a good thing he's living with me, because after a certain point I can tell him (as someone in the same field probably wouldn't), "Enough! I'm not interested in hearing any more about this!" But what can I do when something happens in the hospital that leaves him depressed all night? His attitude is, "I can't have fun when So-and-so is assaultive. I wonder if he's assaulting anyone now. Maybe I should call in and see." Well, when I'm spending the night in the same bed with him, I pick up the same attitude. When he's burned out, I'm burned out.

In this domestic contagion the family stagnates along with the individual.

More serious effects occur when the pressure of overwork destroys or seriously damages personal relationships or keeps a person from forming relationships at all. It would be a mistake, however, to portray the person as an innocent victim of the "system." One *chooses* to live in a small world—whether because one is captivated by the allure of the job, because one is not sufficiently aware of the consequences and the alternatives, or because one does not have much of a personal life in the first place. A social worker in her 30s who by her own testimony "really only wanted to get married since I was about 18" found herself working 60 to 70 hours a week at a rural home for adolescent girls. "Working all the time keeps me from worrying about what's going to happen to me," she explained. "It keeps me from thinking, 'What am I doing out here in the boondocks at my age?'" In a case like this it is hard to tell the chicken from the egg. The job is both the prison and the escape.

There is a cyclic relationship between doing too much on

the job and not doing enough elsewhere. It begins in some cases with a desire to escape from or compensate for an unsatisfactory personal situation. But whether or not one's personal life is impoverished prior to one's self-immersion in the job, it will tend to become so afterward. In the words of a school psychologist, "Yes, I take the job home with me, so much so that I find I don't have time for the give-and-take of an intimate relationship. All I can do is take."

Margaret B., the schoolteacher quoted earlier in this chapter who gave up teaching in response to the demoralizing negativism of her colleagues and supervisors, echoes this sentiment:

> I now realize that I thought of my marriage as an intrusion on my work life. The compelling need I felt to "prove myself" and achieve excellence in the classroom in spite of all obstacles ate away at every relationship I had. At that time I lived by a principle of "psychic energy conservation," whereby the energy that might have gone into building good relationships was deflected into my work. As it was, I didn't even know what a good relationship—that is, a relationship between equals—was. All I could be was either top dog, as I was with the dependent children in school, or underdog, as I was with my husband at home.

With Margaret we see the cycle go one step further. Not having had enough of herself left over to give to her personal relationships, she could not get enough back from them when she needed them for support:

> When I was thwarted in what I wanted to achieve in school, I had no one to turn to anywhere else. I had burned all those bridges. Because I hadn't made the considerable effort it would have taken to work on my relationship with my husband, I could not look to him for any more meaningful support than his sending me off to another man who practiced dominance in the guise of psychiatry. And I didn't have a network of friendships to counteract the negative messages I heard about myself at school. The positive support I got was a whisper next to the cacophany of "You're wrong; you need to change."

This is the destructive cycle of stagnation. The very conditions that create conflicts on the job act to prevent one from building up the reciprocal emotional ties with other people (what a social worker would call "support systems") that would give one greater strength for coping with those conflicts.

When people whose lives are taken up by a job do look for personal relationships, where can they look? As one of the after-work imbibers from the psychiatric ward at Center City Hospital put it,

> With the crazy hours we work and the intensity of our involvement with patients, who else could support us, who else could understand, who else could put up with us but another one of *us?* Only somebody who's in the same boat could accept the way we have to get together on the run. Only another one of us could understand the things we get depressed about. That's why, at least during our first year or so here, just about all our social and sexual gratification comes from the others in the group.

People are forced back on others in the same field for the modicum of human contact they need to keep going. A group language develops, and it becomes hard to speak with people outside the field who do not share the same all-consuming workaday concerns. The small world expands from the after-work drink to evening-long parties, as doctors, lawyers, nurses, teachers, policemen, and social workers (whether or not from the same agency) socialize in the company of those who know the same language and complain about the same problems. To quote once again the wife of a psychiatric nurse:

> Once I thought about inviting a friend of mine to one of Jeff's State Mental Hospital parties, just so I could have somebody to talk to. But why would I subject my friend to that? All they talk about there is State Mental. The last time I went to one of those parties, I was fed up to here with State Mental. So every time someone I was introduced to would ask, "How are you?" I'd smile and say, "Oh, I'm suicidal." "Oh, that's fine," they would say, and introduce me to the next person. They couldn't deal with it.

Her spoof dramatizes what in other contexts is yet another very real frustration of the harried "helper" who only wants to find a few peaceful minutes away from the job: the friends, relatives, and even strangers who "lean on" the off-duty professional for services ranging from the dressing of wounds to marriage counseling. This encroachment on one's life by the ever-enlarging "small world" is, however (like all the others that we have discussed), one's own responsibility to accept or avoid.

Isolated Situations

The boundaries of the "small world" normally are invisible ones; they consist of long hours along with the emotionally draining intensity of the job. There are, however, certain special cases where the boundaries are physical. Geographical isolation is one of these, as in the case of the social worker who worked at an exhausting pace to avoid having to ask herself what she was doing "out in the middle of nowhere." If one has few leisure hours, it is all the worse when there is nothing happening close by. When there are no friends around to see, no new people to meet, who is there to socialize with but fellow staff members— or clients?

The most isolated situation is the live-in facility. There one is placed in a "total environment" whose influence extends not only to professional values and behavior but to the personal sphere as well. Chapter 3 contained the story of Catherine Y., a young college-educated counselor without professional training who worked with female adolescent delinquents. Catherine made the common mistake of identifying too closely with these girls. In their problems with boyfriends and overeating she saw too readily a reflection of her own. How did she come to associate so closely with the young people she was counseling? Coming from a college environment where she estimated that "three-quarters of one's time was social time," she was required to spend her days and nights at a correctional facility. She was given two days a week off, and these were not usually Saturday and Sunday. Socially, she was stranded, left in a vacuum. She filled the vacuum by overidentifying with her clients, being a "big sister" to them, commiserating with them, becoming emotionally involved in their successes and failures—and thus compromising her services to them. Yet, it is entirely understandable that she became "one of the girls." She *did* have some of the same problems they did. She was imprisoned in that institution just as they were.

A form of isolation that affects the person at the other end of the ladder—the fully trained professional—is private practice. As an option open to psychiatrists, psychologists, physicians, attorneys, and social workers, private practice has many attractive features. The person planning to leave a salaried job to set up a practice can look forward to likely benefits such as higher income, less paper work, greater autonomy and control, flexibility in setting hours and choosing clients, and greater appreciation by clients. But a surprising number of people who *are* in private practice cite "isolation" and even "loneliness" as a major source of frustration. They miss the social "breaks" that are built into the day's work at an institution, the intellectual give-and-take with their colleagues at the university. One psychologist mentioned that the isolation of private practice (added to long hours on the job) made her more vulnerable sexually to patients. Her world, like Catherine's, consisted of herself and her patients.

This is one reason why many professionals who could make more money by spending all their time seeing clients instead take part-time faculty appointments at a university or consulting positions with private or government agencies. Others take care of their need for day-to-day personal and intellectual exchange by establishing group practices. Others give themselves enough time off to have an active social life. Without some such intervention, the professional in a private office is in a position not much different (in this one respect) from that of the drug counselor at a live-in rehabilitation clinic who sees few people from the outside world except the ones called "outpatients."

Yet, whatever problems of stagnation the move into private practice may create, it, like other steps toward professional advancement, is seen as a way out of what is often a deadlier form of stagnation. For at the heart of stagnation lies the feeling that one's career is at a dead end.

Chapter 5

CAREER DEAD END

Let's return to Roger F., the "quintessential enthusiast" portrayed in Chapter 3. Roger was a one-time heroin user, not long out of treatment himself, who lived and worked at a drug rehabilitation clinic during its early, experimental years. At the beginning he ran groups with an innocent fervor that rubbed off on the addicts he worked with. "I quivered with pride in what I was doing. Nothing else mattered . . . All my strokes came from the job."

Where was he six months later? Still spending 60 hours a week seeing clients on an assembly-line basis without having been taught how to distinguish those who were likely to benefit from his efforts from those who were not. Still living at the facility and earning $39.50 a week plus room and board. By then he was beginning to want an apartment of his own and a car for getting around the city, but how could he hope to get those things on his salary? And without a decent income, without the apartment, without the car, he was "grounded" socially —unless he approached one of the many women addicts who came to the clinic for help. That was what some of the other counselors were doing. Roger saw the hanky panky that was going on among the counselors, such as drinking on the job, fraternizing with addict clients of the opposite sex, and buying "hot" tires and TV sets from clients. Roger himself did not do those things—yet. But he sensed that if he stayed in that place long enough, he would come to live as the others lived.

He saw that he could not make it as a counselor, and that he could never make it if he stayed a counselor. This realization was crystallized by one incident:

> I once was asked to speak at a clinical conference, where a representative of each therapeutic discipline reported on some aspect of a patient's case. A scribe was there to take notes. A psychiatrist introduced the case: "Twenty-six year old, white, married male. . . ." The scribe took down what he said. A nurse reported, "Medication is being administered q.i.d. Adaptation to the ward has been good." A psychologist said, "Psychological tests show that no organicity is present." A social worker spoke about "family history" and "significant others." All the while the scribe took notes. When I rose to speak for the counseling staff, the scribe went to the bathroom.

The next day Roger reported the slight to the director of the clinic, who told him, "You can't expect what you fellas say to be taken seriously. You fellas are semi-patients here yourselves, you know." That made it clear to Roger that there was no career for him at that agency. As a paraprofessional counselor he would always remain an underpaid quasi-patient patronized by the professional staff and subjected to periodic urinalyses to check for drug use. It was a dead end.

LOW PAY

Low pay, the most tangible sign of career dead end, is a major focus of discontent in the helping professions. It gives people the feeling that their choices in life are constrained, their scope of activity narrowed. How can someone live a "decent" or "normal" life (whether that is defined as dating and going out with friends or buying a home and supporting a family) on what seems, and may well be, little more than a subsistence income? A mental health technician captured the essence of stagnation when he opened his weekly pay envelope and said, "There's got to be more to life than this."

Admittedly there are wide variations in pay within the human services, as there are elsewhere. Still, when people who work in the field talk about Burn-out, there is no issue that is more frequently raised than "low pay." It is true that this is a concrete issue that is easier to articulate than some of the subtler frustrations of the trade. And it may simply be the case that Americans in general are preoccupied with money and find numerous reasons to think that they are not being paid enough. Yet there is, if anything, a greater-than-usual concern about the issue in the helping professions—and for good reason.

The preoccupation extends from the lowest pay and status levels to the highest. Understandably, it is most acute among paraprofessionals. Although the days of the $39.50-a-week state employee (usually a recovering addict who was expected to be grateful that he was given a job at all) are over, it is questionable whether the pay scales of most paraprofessionals have risen much more steeply than the rate of inflation of the dollar. "Street savvy" does not buy much bread in our degree-oriented economy. One of the benefits of the steps taken by drug and alcohol rehabilitation programs in the 1970s to upgrade the status of the paraprofessional by training recovering addicts and alcoholics *before* allowing them to work with clients is that the person who is trained to assume more responsibility can command a higher rate of pay. Nonetheless, low pay remains a prime cause of the high turnover rate among paraprofessionals. A person who has any of the normal material aspirations of Americans (or just the aspiration to have a family) will not be able to make a go of it as a paraprofessional. Even someone who likes the job will have to move on. It is a temporary job, a stepping stone to higher things.

The college-educated "helper" without professional credentials may not be much better off. Certainly, such a person almost always earns more than an untrained paraprofessional.

But he or she also *expects* more, and the higher expectation can virtually cancel out the higher remuneration. The phenomenon of "rising expectations" is clearly illustrated in the case of a person who made the transition from the lowest-paid group to the next higher category. Jack F. had no complaints about his pay as an addiction counselor, since it put more money in his pocket than he had ever had during his years out on the street as an addict. As he saw himself promoted from counselor I to counselor II and then counselor III, he had every reason to be satisfied. It was only after he obtained his undergraduate degree that he began to consider himself underpaid. For now, instead of contrasting his present situation with his disadvantaged past, he could compare himself to the average educated American. This is, of course, the standard against which college-educated human services workers who are not former addicts or prison inmates measure themselves from the start.

Nor does the financial insecurity, the envy, the jockeying for a better position cease at the higher professional levels. There we see a social worker in the family services institute, a woman with a master's degree in the field, preparing to go into private practice because she expects that she will earn more money there than at the state-funded institute. Meanwhile, a clinical psychologist who *is* in private practice finds her position, for several reasons, a precarious one:

> No question about it, private practice is demanding. If I don't produce, I don't make money. No salaried security, no paid vacations here. If I lose a patient, I'm also losing thirty dollars a week until I get another patient for that hour. At the beginning I had trouble seeing my patients objectively because I needed them as much as they needed me. As a result I wasn't a good judge of whether or not they should stay in therapy. And even now I wonder if I'm being hypocritical when I advise patients to take paid sick leave when necessary from their salaried jobs, while I come to work sick because I would lose the day's fees if I cancelled my appointments. I get angry at patients who don't pay their bills, because then I feel that my work has been all

output and no intake—which I guess says something I might not like to admit about the other satisfactions I get from my work.

What makes people feel that they are or (more often) are not making enough money? How do people decide how much money they "should" be making? What yardsticks do they measure their income against? Here are some of the most commonly invoked standards of comparison:

One's Own Needs

The most straightforward way to decide how much money one should be making is to figure out how much it costs to live what one considers a decent life. One's needs do tend to evolve, though, as one grows older and accumulates time in the job. At first, just doing the job may seem like not only a decent life, but a wonderful one. But as enthusiasm wears off and one reaches a different stage of personal development, other needs come to the fore. Frank V., who left the priesthood after 12 years to become a social worker, recounts the evolution of his own needs as he explains the difficulties he has found in assigning himself a secular market value:

> As a counselor in the court system I started at the bottom of the pay scale even though I had a master's degree and years of experience in counseling people as a priest. That was okay as long as my wife was working and we had no children. But once my wife left her job and we began to have a family, I realized that I needed more income. And after 12 years of serving people without expecting any return, I felt that my services were worth something. No longer did I have to sacrifice to help people. But just how much was I worth?

Compared to other vocations, there is a disproportionately large number of people in the human services who, like Frank, took their first "real job" in their 30s. Until then, for one of several possible reasons, they were outside the labor market.

Some of them were priests, nuns, or their counterparts in other faiths. Some were in jails or treatment facilities. Some were in schools working toward graduate degrees. All of these people, whether overeducated or undereducated, lived under the protection of institutions of one sort or another prior to beginning work in the helping field. There are also many alcoholic refugees from business or other careers who switched to counseling at an even more advanced age. These individuals have had to adjust to a different (usually lower) pay scale, as well as to the fact that they are being paid for a new set of skills. (Lee Silverstein, author of *Consider the Alternative,*[1] who obtained his M.S.W. degree after a highly successful career in the insurance business, tells how he could not get used to the idea of accepting money from people in return for listening and talking to them.) People who do not begin work in the field until relatively late in life are often particularly unsure of their value in the job market and somewhat tentative in establishing their position there.

But they are not the only ones who face Frank's question: "What am I worth?" which along with "What good am I doing?" (or "What *am* I doing?") is one of the central dilemmas of the helping professional. Everyone faces it at some point. Everyone has some idea of the value society attaches (or *should* attach) to the job one does. The answer to this question is compounded of a number of factors, including one's training, competence, experience, and capacity to assume responsibility. Ultimately, though, this answer cannot be found in a vacuum. It is found by looking around and making comparisons with others, and that is where what Frank calls the "emotional dimension" (i.e., the sense of grievance) comes into the picture.

Comparisons with Clients

Frank goes on to describe some wayward thoughts he has had while sitting across the desk from a well-heeled client:

> Here I am counseling somebody who is making $30,000 a year, while I'm only making $9000. I know that person isn't worth

what he's getting, and yet here I am helping him pull in all that money. It certainly doesn't make me feel easy about what I'm getting for my work. Once I start using other people's pay as a yardstick for my own, once I start comparing their abilities, qualifications, and responsibilities with mine, I find my needs (subjectively, that is) increasing. Then I'm no longer simply being pragmatic; I'm getting emotionally invested in the issue, and I'm jeopardizing my enjoyment of my work. I have to catch myself and let go of that resentment, or else I won't be happy doing anything, for there will always be someone I can find to envy.

Indeed there will be. A clinical psychologist who earns the $30,000 that Frank envies, and who has clients who earn even more, has a good answer for Frank:

How can I envy them when all I have to do is remind myself why they are there to see me? That money isn't making them happy. It doesn't enable them to have better lives than I have. I can't envy a big businessman who is impotent or dependent on alcohol.

Comparisons with Those who Have Higher-Paying Jobs in the Same Field

It is only natural for people to compare their pay with that of the people who work beside them—and above them. Most people are more interested in seeing how they stack up against those in higher positions than against those who rank below them. This is especially true wherever there is a discrepancy between formal status distinctions and actual skills and responsibilities. "Here we are working right with these people and doing the same things they are, and they make twice as much as we do." It was a mental health worker who spoke these words, and he was talking about the psychiatric nurses in his unit. But it might just as well have been the psychiatric nurses talking about the psychiatrists. And as in the medical system, so it is also in the legal field. A family services caseworker complained, "I'm the one who has to make the tough decisions that affect the welfare of families. The lawyers and judges, who just rubber-stamp my recommendations, are the ones who divvy up the spoils." Front-line workers feel that they, not their better-paid, titled superiors, are the ones who understand the problems of clients. Lower-level administrators feel that they, not top management, are the ones who really manage the staff. And so on up the line. At any level one can find good reasons (if one so chooses) to feel inadequately rewarded for one's contribution. And hovering in the background is an issue that will be considered more fully in Chapter 8—the fact that there are more women in the low-paying jobs and more men in the high-paying ones.

Comparisons with the Private Sector

The private sector is the tantalizing alternative, the "might have been" that may actually have been in one's past and may still be in one's future. "What if I had been like my best friend," one muses, "and gone to work for Honeywell or IBM? Maybe it's not too late to do it yet." Nearly everyone in the human services has a few real-life *alter egos* (often old school friends) who have chosen other vocations. Against their accomplishments one can measure one's own success. After a number of years in the field, the comparison usually is to the disadvantage of the person in the helping professions—and not just the person who has only an undergraduate degree. The following comment by an M.S.W. working in a hospital alcoholism unit is representative of what individuals at all pay and status levels experience. "Representative" is perhaps too weak a word; it is almost a verbatim echo of what many others have said:

> After four years on the job I am making only $13,000 a year. I'll admit that my friends who do not have professional positions envy me, but my friends in other professions make twice as much as I do! Their skills, their contributions are not so much better than mine as to justify that differential.

One does not even have to think up these comparisons oneself. They are constantly forced on one by friends and relatives who say, "I told you so." A key factor in one's commitment to working in the human services is the support one gets from important people in one's life. Often that support is not forthcoming. The low levels of pay in the human services in part create and in part reflect the lack of prestige of those occupations in our society. This lack of prestige stems from what is thought to be their irrelevance to a productive economy. It has other sources as well, among them the inherent unmeasurability of the work itself. Here we have the testimony of several individuals whose spouses, parents, and close associates question the value (monetary and otherwise) of what they are doing for a living:

1. A woman with a B.A. in sociology who counsels alcoholics: "My family has always been well off. My father, who is an engineer, doesn't like what I'm doing. He thinks it's a 'dirty job.' "

2. A woman who gave up a promising academic career to counsel troubled adolescents: "I'm constantly dipping into my own pocket to pay for things for the kids. Obviously I can't do that forever. But it's not just that it's hard to live on two-thirds of my previous salary; it's that my family doesn't respect my work. All the time they tell me, 'Here you're a Ph.D., and you're making half as much as your cousins with B.A.s.' Friends tell me the same thing. They define the value of work solely by the salary that comes with it. I hate to have to keep defending what I'm doing."

3. A woman who went directly from college into an M.S.W. program and has remained a professional social worker: "Not that my husband doesn't support me or respect what I'm doing, but he does like to say that I don't have a 'regular job' because all I do is 'chat with people.' "

4. A man with an M.A. in sociology who counsels prison inmates: "I'm glad my wife has supported me in my career decisions, because no one else has. My parents

don't really understand what this work is all about. And my aunt once said to me, 'Why don't you get a *good* job—like state trooper?' "

In a society oriented toward action, what does it mean to talk to people? In a society that values achievement, what does it mean to help those who have not achieved? In a materialistic society, what does it mean to have a low-paying job?

The Pluses and Minuses

There is, nonetheless, a compensatory benefit in working for the local, state, or federal government (as a good many people in the human services do), namely, job security. The man whose aunt would like him to be a state trooper has a good-humored grasp of the seductive advantages of civil service:

> Once you start getting those fringe benefits from the state, it's as if they "got 'cha." It's a little frightening to me now to think about getting a job in private industry. My next-door neighbor works for one of the big insurance companies. He has a good job, and he certainly makes more than I do, but once in a while it must hit him that he could get laid off. I don't have to worry about that—not as long as people continue to get busted!

Ultimately, one has to make a value judgment about whether it is worthwhile to work in a low-paying field. A counselor in one of the armed services who is approaching retirement age has made that judgment for himself:

> In the service, where pay scales are standardized, I didn't lose anything financially by transferring from technical work to counseling. That will no longer be the case when I retire and go into civilian life. There I could get two or three times as much money in a technical field. But I'll sacrifice that for the other satisfactions I get from working with people.

Someone else, with equal validity, might make the opposite choice.

DEAD ENDS THROUGHOUT THE HIERARCHY

The theme of the career dead end comes through strongly in the accounts of paraprofessionals like Roger F. who lack formal training. Another counselor in the drug and alcohol field puts it this way: "After a while I saw that I wasn't really being listened to by the clients or the professionals. They were both using me as a middleman, an interpreter to help them understand each other's languages. It made me feel left out." A colleague of his adds:

> We got it from both ends of the stick. The professionals were compensated for overtime and rewarded for doing more work or better work; we weren't. Even the patients had better prospects than we did. All the attention was lavished on them, not us. They were getting stipends to go to school while we stayed right where we were."

There could hardly be a more striking image of stagnation.

Underlying these grievances are some of the frustrations whose implications we will consider in subsequent chapters, such as "powerlessness," "no support for important decisions," or "bad office politics." The feeling of being at a dead end in one's career is a feeling of having no status, no power, no "say." What the scribe's behavior told Roger was that his case report had no official standing, i.e., that what he had to say did not matter. This sort of bureaucratic putdown is bound to strike a raw nerve, and not only in Roger's case. "The counselors wrote reports for the patients' charts," complains another paraprofessional, "and then they couldn't get into the charts to see their own reports." A woman whose two-year associate's degree brought her into alcoholism treatment and family counseling ostensibly at higher than a paraprofessional level found herself regularly excluded from staff meetings at the institutions where she worked.

Career dead end is an issue whose impact on those in the lower professional strata is evident. It is of special concern to those who are at a disadvantage in education and hierarchical status. The psychiatric technician bristles at the notion of "custodial" duties, preferring instead to see himself working in a therapeutic capacity. But such feelings are by no means limited to paraprofessionals, since the sense of being at a disadvantage arises from one's expectations rather than one's objective position. Everyone feels at a disadvantage when looking up. Nurses, who have professional status (Roger would have been happy to have been the nurse who spoke at the clinical conference), are quick to express resentment against physicians for discounting their suggestions and not allowing them any say in treatment decisions. And then there was the man with a master's degree in clinical psychology whose first job in a prestigious psychiatric hospital consisted of administering psychological tests without being consulted when the results were interpreted. He was in much the same position as the drug counselor who was denied access to his own reports in the patients' records. He had to move on.

The two top administrators of a vocational training agency established with Office of Economic Opportunity funds in the 1960s have experienced a career dead end of a different sort from Roger's humiliation at the clinical conference. For them the dead end is "managerial obsolescence." The director originally was given his position in much the same way as a recovering addict is designated a "counselor"; as an unemployed executive, he himself had been one of the program's first applicants for vocational aid. He hired as his assistant a recent college graduate with no previous work experience and they started the office with "a pad and pencil, a card table, and an account book." Over the next decade, despite cutbacks in other social service areas, reducing unemployment remained a high priority of the government. The program grew until it had a staff of 35 and a 5 million dollar budget. Its growth was a natural consequence of the allocation of government funds on a nationwide basis. It was only natural, though, for the director and his assistant to give themselves credit for nurturing "their" local agency from birth to maturity. In fact, they had little aptitude for managing a large, complex organization such as their "baby" had become.

With its expanded budget and manpower, the agency attracted more attention and scrutiny from the government. Recently a reorganization plan "came down" from Washington. The director and assistant director kept their jobs, but a new slot was created above the assistant director and a new person brought in to fill it. The reorganization, a belated acknowledgment of the vast expansion of the program, has not taken any responsibilities away from the assistant director. She still has the same job to do. Objectively, nothing has changed for her. Subjectively, everything has changed.

This administrator has been stagnating without realizing it. Still working at her first job, she has not learned many new skills over the past decade. All along, though, she has derived a sensation of progress from the evolution of the organization and a feeling of security from her unchallenged place within it. She might have been happy to stay there forever. Now she has been given a jolt. Like Roger at the clinical conference, she has seen the limitations of her position publicly exposed. All the questions she has never had to ask herself now have to be answered. Essentially, she has three options. She can become frustrated and apathetic, risking loss of effectiveness and perhaps loss of the job itself. She can go on doing her job as well as she always has (perhaps an easier task objectively than subjectively). Or she can broaden her experience by applying for jobs in other agencies.

The director, too, must be asking himself some questions. He has just been shown that no one is safe; everyone is vulnerable. What may happen to his own position?

The Dilemmas of Career Advancement

The feeling that one's career is at a dead end can come to almost anyone at any time. As Gail Sheehy has shown in *Passages,*[2] it is natural at certain points in life to reevaluate one's situation critically. And as we shall see in the following chapter, frustration over the issues of power and status works both ways. If a recovering alcoholic working at a rehabilitation center is given second-class treatment as a "quasi-patient," a bright-eyed college graduate who is *not* an alcoholic may not get a job there at all or may not be fully accepted by the other counselors. The nurse or medical aide who would like to have more influence over the decisions of doctors and hospital administrators probably does not realize that people in high positions can find themselves equally powerless to influence the behavior of subordinates.

In its most typical form, though, career dead end strikes the front-line worker who genuinely wants to help people but lacks the wherewithal to do so effectively. This theme is most clearly articulated by Warren C., who came into the field of correctional counseling in his mid-20s with an undergraduate education in sociology and a tour of duty in Vietnam behind him:

> Yes, I wanted more money; yes, I suppose everyone enjoys exercising more power. But in great part my decision to try to rise in the organization was an expression of my original idealism. I came in wanting to change the corrections department; I wanted to be a part of something new and exciting. As I became enmeshed in what was going on, I realized that if I wanted to play a significant part, if I wanted to have a hand in new developments, I would have to do it from a position of greater responsibility.

The person who reaches a dead end can do one of two things. One is to dig out a comfortable rut and stay in it. But it is not always easy to still the inner voice of protest against stagnation, the voice that cries, "There's got to be more to life than this." The alternative is to try to move up in the agency or in the profession. This course, too, has its drawbacks and complications. Someone who seeks to rise in the field faces two major obstacles to advancement—obstacles or opportunities, that is, depending on how one looks at them.

Need for Academic Credentials

The first requirement for advancement in many fields is further education. Throughout the helping professions there is an increasing emphasis on academic degrees as prerequisites for hiring or promotion. It was not too long ago that a college degree was not thought to have much to do with police work. Now police departments actively court each year's graduating class, and officers on the force are under more and more pressure to go back and get their degrees. Similarly, it used to be that anyone who could read and write could become a mental health aide. However, today hospital administrators prefer college graduates. The nursing profession is undergoing something of a revolution as the B.S. degree is being recognized as a necessary supplement to the RN for promotion beyond a front-line position. And it is not so easy as it was a decade ago to become a drug or alcohol counselor with no more than a degree from the "school of hard knocks" (i.e., a personal history of substance abuse).

Some people take these requirements in stride, welcoming the opportunity for self-improvement. The psychologist with an M.A. who was stuck in a dead-end job administering tests got himself unstuck by getting his Ph.D. Warren C., the correctional counselor who wanted more say in running the prison system, had some free schooling coming to him as a veteran's benefit. So he obtained *two* master's degrees—one in public administration so that he could learn administrative skills and qualify for advancement, and one in sociology so that he could have more front-line involvement with inmates.

Not everyone, however, is so agreeable to the demands of

the system. An element of frustration enters the picture when academic degree requirements are perceived as artificial, as bureaucratic "mickeymouse" that disregards experience and talent. This complaint is heard frequently from nurses who, in their impatience to get out onto the hospital floors and tend to sick people, become RNs, signifying practical competence in nursing, only to find later that they need a B.S. to get them *off* the floors. Many people who take the required degrees do so with a certain cynicism, admitting that it is something they have to do for advancement even though the training program leading to the degree has little relevance to their work. Others express bitterness at having to go through an empty ritual. A woman whose vast experience in dealing with people on and off the job did not become marketable until she earned an M.S.W. degree has this to say:

> Given the time my academic training took from my actual work in the field as well as from my life, I hoped that it would have some practical value. It did not. Clinical, experiential training is much more valuable, but without the degree it is not accepted as adequate preparation. I resent having been forced to get a paper degree.

Finally, there is the sceptical voice that says that it all does not matter so much anyway. Looking up at the layers of more highly qualified people above him, one psychiatric technician was not impressed. "So what if I'm no longer enthusiastic," he remarked. "The nurses and the social workers get frustrated, too. From what I can see, they don't look all that happy, either. So I wouldn't put much stock in added credentials unless I were going to go all the way to the top and become a psychiatrist."

Where he would find some of the highest rates of alcoholism, drug addiction, divorce, and suicide.

The Administrative Route to Promotion

For the person who comes into the helping professions (as most do) to work directly with people, it is frustrating to learn that the surest and sometimes the only route to advancement is not through front-line involvement with clients, but through supervisory and administrative work. In teaching, in nursing, in social work, accepting a promotion generally entails working less with people and more with official forms, budgets, and subordinate staff members. In the military services, too, career growth opportunities are limited unless one becomes an officer (i.e., a manager).

An irritated head nurse whose heart was still back with her patients on the ward recalled, "What excited me about nursing was that I was out there doing things for people. I don't want to keep a lot of silly records for the state." Not only did her promotion take her away from her patients; it took her away from her peers as well. When she tried to maintain her involvement with patients as well as with the staff by continuing to do the "little things" she had always done out on the floor (while having to keep up with her desk work at the same time), her former co-workers asked her, "What are you doing out here helping us?" They saw her as usurping their place; she saw herself as still wanting to be one of them.

Alienation from former peers is often reported by supervisors who rise from the ranks, like this drug counselor:

> Other counselors who were promoted to counselor II did not become more professional in their approach. I did. I wanted to get some new things done, and I made demands on the people under me. Some of them were threatened by this. The talk in the halls would stop when I came around. So now I am no longer really friends with these people, but I still can't hang out with the professionals.

A nurse and a mental health worker who were made supervisors of their respective departments on a hospital psychiatric ward found themselves in the same no-man's-land:

> We're both no longer "one of the gang," and there's some resentment of our status. This on top of the fact that we're blamed for everything by the supervisors, we don't have any power to implement our decisions, and we aren't being paid more for taking on these responsibilities. Why did we do it, anyway?

There, in a nutshell, is the range of problems that may be faced by the newly promoted supervisor. That a more balanced appraisal is possible is suggested by a social worker who gives a good account of the dilemma and of her own response to it:

> Some years ago there used to be a position in my department called psychiatric social worker II, where you got a raise even though you did not become an administrator. That has been abolished. So I did the only thing that was left to do; I took on one B.A.-level social worker as a trainee and assistant. One day I woke up and found two more assigned to me, plus a college student for the summer. Being responsible for them has taken a tremendous amount of energy. But I must say I've realized some new strengths in the process.

Warren C. has faced the same dilemma in the prison system. "The higher you go in the bureaucracy," he noted, "the more paper work you get. I'm often tempted to go back to the front lines. But I'm not sure how to move 'backwards' like that without losing the pay and the position I've achieved." With his degrees in sociology and public administration, however, Warren has given himself maneuvering room within the organization. When he found himself getting stale after a few months as director of a program that he had helped create, he gave up the post and went into staff development, where he could "work with the people who work with people." It was a constructive intervention, a way around the administrative dilemma.

A CASE OF STAGNATION

Jean Q. became a nurse because she felt that nurses "had a certain dignity about them." The Clara Barton image was reinforced by the nurses she met in person as well as in books and on TV (where she liked the look of the nurses' caps in the soap operas). Jean imagined that she would enjoy the challenge of an intense, busy situation.

As an RN she began work in a 40-bed male surgical unit in a large city hospital. Each shift was handled by two nurses and two orderlies. She had not expected the place to be so understaffed. The heavy work load kept her from doing the "little things" to comfort patients as she had learned to do in nursing school. She had been taught, for example, that each patient should have a daily back rub. Now she felt fortunate when she could get all the dressings changed.

In nursing school Jean had learned what ought to be done, other things being equal. What she had not learned was what to do if other things were not equal. She had not been taught *triage*. When you do not have the resources (time, for example) to do everything that ought to be done, how do you set priorities? Which conditions require prompt attention? Which patients can benefit from some attention? Without some such guidelines she wore herself thin. She was doing a lot more than she was being paid for. "This isn't what I thought it would be like," she said to herself.

Jean had never had much use for alcohol, let alone drugs. Now, however, she began to hang out with the medical students at the hospital, who introduced her to tranquilizers and sleeping pills. Once at a party she mentioned to one of the students that she was having trouble sleeping. He gave her a few Nembutals. "Whatever gets you through the night," he said.

She liked the feeling she got from the drug. Good feelings were what she was looking for, since for some time she had "felt something lacking" on the job. She was working hard and well, but she was never thanked or praised for her efforts by the doctors or patients (least of all by her fellow nurses, who never seemed to give themselves or each other enough credit). The work "left her a little empty at times." She did not get the lift she would have expected after taking care of people all day.

Still, she did not take Nembutal again until her roommate moved out a few months later. Now living alone, she found it harder and harder to get to sleep. The Nembutal was right there (in bottles of a thousand, of which no inventories were kept) on the medicine cart that she wheeled around the ward at night. If a patient complained of sleeplessness, she thought nothing of giving him a Nembutal. She thought nothing of slipping a few into her own pocket as well. For months she took at least one every night. Meanwhile, she found that she had no trouble obtaining prescriptions from doctors for everything from Percodan to Demerol, from muscle relaxants to Dilaudid.

For several years she stayed on the job while using drugs. From all indications she was functioning quite adequately, but sometimes she was not sure. She could not always remember at the end of the day whether all the patients had received the right medications. At times the only RN on the ward, she was expected to give care and comfort to every patient while making decisions that she did not always feel competent to make. She was exhausted, physically and mentally. She felt that she was not getting anywhere. There were days when she hated to go to work.

Jean's drug use finally was exposed when a succession of physical collapses and lapses of memory caused her to be hospitalized. After receiving treatment she eventually returned to nursing in the drug and alcohol field. Her case is a prime instance of stagnation in a front-line helping professional. For Jean, drug use appears to have filled the gap between expectations and reality. It helped her forget that a nurse was supposed to be dignified, respected, and happy, when in fact she was pressured and put down.

The other key feature of stagnation that Jean's case illustrates is the spread of a deviant pattern of coping within a permissive social environment. People in many trades and professions experience the strain of overwork and the discrepancy between expectation and reality. Medical professionals and trainees are among the most likely to resolve these conflicts by using drugs because drugs are available and socially acceptable in their milieu. In the course of their work doctors and nurses see what drugs are for, what effects they have, and why people use them. That is how they are socialized into a mode of behavior that is controversial in the outside world and that in some respects is clearly harmful.

In the self-destructive behavior and debilitating physical symptoms that Jean developed in response to the pressures and dissatisfactions of her work, we also see a preview of the next stage of Burn-out. Stagnation, we recall, occurs when you still feel that you are doing the job, but begin to question what the job is doing for you. What happens when you question whether you are really even doing the job?

Chapter 6

POLITICS AND POWERLESSNESS

Frustration. We think of the 2-year-old stamping his foot and burying his head in a pillow because some bright object that has caught his eye remains out of his reach. Our frustrations take longer to build up. We take longer to react to them, too, and they take a different kind of toll on us.

Frustration is the core of Burn-out. In the stage of frustration, people who have set out to give others what they need find that they themselves are not getting what they want. They are not doing the job they set out to do. They are not "really helping." Leaving aside the low pay, long hours, and low status, there is a more basic frustration in the helping professions. It is inherently difficult to change people, and it is even more difficult under currently prevalent working conditions.

Frustration can be experienced as a sudden blow, a moment of stark enlightenment, as in the case of the Air Force alcoholism counselor who thought he could cure the guy nobody else on base could do anything for—thought he *had* cured him, until he found him hospitalized on another base. Or it can sink in over a period of time, leaving a person with what one counselor called "a feeling of inner emptiness and doubt, a feeling that nothing was going on for me."

Here is how Roger F., the drug counselor, describes frustration. When we last saw Roger, he was stagnating, his career path blocked. Within a matter of months he was to pass into the next stage of Burn-out:

> For a while I carried on even though I knew already that I couldn't do it all. It didn't matter that I didn't believe in the system as long as I believed in myself. As far as I was concerned, supervisors and administrators were there for one reason only— to keep me from helping people. After all, I had all the answers.
>
> Then I started asking myself where were all the people I was supposed to be helping. Continually relapsing? Letting me down? Ripping me off? Trying to bribe or seduce me? I felt powerless, put upon, as if the bureaucracy was putting me out as cannon fodder to face the hassles and threats from the addicts who came in off the street every day.
>
> Someone once sent me a letter telling me how much I had helped him and how I had changed his life. I carried that letter around with me for several weeks, until I saw a newspaper article saying that the guy had been given three to five years for armed robbery.

After that Roger carried around the article in place of the letter. He wanted a constant reminder of the lesson of detachment that he had learned from his initial frustrations.

There is a 12-point planning board exercise that has proved very useful in identifying issues of concern to people. A person is given a blank piece of 8 in. X 11 in. paper and asked to tear it into 12 parts. On each of the first 11 sheets the person writes one of the common frustrations in the help-giving fields, as dictated by the person administering the exercise. The 12th sheet is left blank as a "Wild Card." Here the person can call attention to any issue not covered in the standard list. After rearranging the slips of paper so as to rank the 12 items in order of importance, the person then describes how he or she experiences each of the 12 frustrations.

People's frustrations have a way of pouring out in response to the exercise. Four of these—"not enough money," "too many hours," "career dead end," and "can't measure success" (one that turns up frequently as a Wild Card choice)—have been covered in our discussion of stagnation. The eight others that make up the standard list (along with some Wild Cards listed in Chapter 8) pertain more to the frustration stage.

Of these, there are two that stand out as, in a sense, encompassing all the rest. Much of the frustration that people run up against in the helping professions is summed up in the phrases "powerlessness" and "system not responsive to clients' needs." The second refers to the expectations people have for clients; the first refers to the expectations people have for themselves. What, after all, are the unrealistic hopes that characterize the stage of enthusiasm? Essentially, they boil down to two: (1) "Clients' lives will be changed," and (2) "I will be the one who will make a difference for them." But if the system is not responsive to clients' needs, how can clients benefit? If one feels powerless, how can one be of service?

These are the two large areas in which reality confounds expectation. Many of the other issues highlighted by the 12-point exercise can, in fact, be looked at as variations of these —i.e., reasons why people can feel powerless and ways in which the system can be unresponsive. We will take up the first group of issues in this chapter and the second in the following chapter.

POWERLESSNESS

The sensation of powerlessness—which is what Burn-out is all about—is experienced at many levels by people in the helping professions. Most obvious is the powerlessness felt by front-line workers who occupy the lowest positions in the decision-making hierarchy, namely, the counselor who has no way to compel her alcoholic clients to keep their appointments with her; the counselor who unsuccessfully seeks educational opportunities and community activities for addicts; the teacher whose proposals for extracurricular cultural enrichment programs are neither explicitly rejected nor approved by the school board.

Powerlessness, however, is relative to one's position. A frequent complaint of supervisors and middle managers is that their subordinates credit them with more power than they actually have. When front-line staff members see their supervisor attend meetings with the bigwigs, they may not believe his assertion that he lacks the authority to get them what they want from management. Actually, although the supervisor may be given every right to speak up at those meetings, his views may have little weight. It is the directors' wishes that carry the day.

What about the director, then? The dean of a university program in community service education speaks about powerlessness in a way that would surprise classroom teachers who complain of their own powerlessness:

> I have confidence in my own judgment in hiring, but I also am responsible for personnel who are hired "for" me by others. I don't choose them, but I'm still accountable for them. And regardless of who hires the teachers, nobody has day-to-day control over them. I can remember back when I myself was a teacher. When I closed the classroom door behind me, I was the boss. Now they close that door on me. No one knows what goes on behind that closed door.
>
> As for institutional power, the fact that an idea originates with me doesn't mean that I can carry it out in anything like its original form—at least not without a hassle that will come back to haunt me the next time I want something from the same people. There are many institutional prerogatives to be respected. It's frustrating, but I can't do much about it, even as dean. Sure, I can make my influence felt, but not when it comes to making big moves, major changes, innovations. An organization as large as this one has become is not about to be moved, not by me any more than by the janitor. More and more I have found that the mold is set. The organization has its own direction.

So much for life at the top.

The feeling of powerlessness is universal; it goes beyond one's hierarchical status. Its broader implications are suggested by one counselor's way of defining it: "Powerlessness means my being unable to change things." "Things" can mean everything from "the system" to human nature, from the family dynamics that engender emotional and behavioral problems to the social conditions that spawn poverty and ignorance. The inability to change any of these "givens," the inability to control clients, subordinates, superiors, the agency, the system—this is the frustration that leads directly to Burn-out. More than one worker in the field has remarked on the chronically corrosive effect that this feeling of impotence has on a person's self-esteem. When one sets out to move mountains only to find that they do not budge, one comes to doubt one's worth—until one realizes that mountains were not made to be moved.

Notwithstanding the idealism that motivates people to enter the helping professions, issues of power and control are central to the helping relationship. Some people complain that they do not have enough power; others (or the same people in different situations) complain that they have too much power. The latter is not the same as being held nominally responsible for results while being denied decision-making authority—just another form of powerlessness. Too much power is another issue altogether. The client in a helping relationship is in a dependent position, and it can be scary to have that dependency focused on oneself, even if one inwardly has sought such power by going into the field in the first place. Carol P., a nurse who dispenses methadone at a drug clinic, has confronted this issue with considerable honesty and penetration. She describes how uncomfortable it makes her to hold the key to someone else's desires:

> I'm the one the addicts have to come to for their goodies. I'm the one who gives out the methadone or withholds it. It's humiliating for them to submit to the check list of requirements that I'm required to put them through before they can get their dose, and it's difficult for me to tell them when they're not eligible for it. They need the stuff, and they have to come to me to get it, so naturally they hate me. They have to take the medication in

my presence, and I even go into the bathroom with them to make sure the urine sample for the urinalysis is an honest one. It's dehumanizing.

Margo J. taught a college course in women's issues so that she might "give women students some new things to think about." The results were surprising and unsettling:

As I went along I tried to assess the value of what I was doing. Was I providing anything that would help other women? I decided—convinced myself, I suppose—that I was. Meanwhile, the women's responses went far beyond my expectations. I was shocked when they came up to me and said, "I just broke my engagement" (or whatever). "You've changed my way of thinking about things." I was horrified at the students' naivete. "Wait a minute, look at what you're doing," I'd tell them. It wasn't at all my intention to convert them, to alter their lives. I just wanted to open up some issues for them to consider. After that I made my lectures less dramatic, less colorful, more like an intellectual exercise. I don't like to feel that I'm having no effect on people, but I also don't like to see people changing their lives because of me.

Who was being naive here? In not realizing that her students would act out the ideas they learned in her class, Margo failed to comprehend her own power as a teacher. When she saw how much responsibility she had unwittingly assumed over others' lives, she backed away from it. Power is an issue that anyone who works with people must confront—not only in terms of how little power one has, but how much as well. One's power has definite limits, and these are frustrating, but the reality of that power can be frustrating as well.

No Support for Important Decisions

Recently in New England there was a great public outcry over a light sentence given to a convicted murderer. This man had pleaded guilty to killing someone with a shotgun after a neighborhood squabble. In a presentence report to the court, a probation officer with six years' experience recommended that the man be placed on probation. The report cited the absence of a previous criminal record or history of violence, along with the man's good employment record and stable family situation. The judge concurred in the recommendation, and the man was released from prison. The victim's family insistently protested that this was too lenient a sentence for such a serious crime. Their cause was taken up by the media and a state investigation followed. In the end, the probation officer was "allowed to resign" from his $10,500-a-year job. The judge kept his $40,000-a-year post.

It is appropriate that public servants be held accountable to the public for their acts. And in this instance there was good reason to question the propriety of the decision that was reached. It is striking, however, that in accepting the probation officer's recommendation, the judge did not (in his own eyes or the public's) accept responsibility for acting upon it. A subordinate who made an unpopular recommendation was held solely accountable for the consequences of its implementation. It was a notable instance of "no support for important decisions."

The probation officer's dilemma can be seen every day in situations that do not make headlines. For instance, a family services worker is asked to work out a divorce settlement. When the couple finds the settlement unsatisfactory, the lawyers disassociate themselves from it and put the onus on the family services worker. Teachers, counselors, social workers find themselves being held responsible for their superiors' failure to back up their recommendations. It is doubly frustrating to see clients go without needed services and to feel oneself unjustly blamed.

More than anyone, though, it is the administrator who cites "no support for important decisions" as a prime frustration. Administrators at all levels are preoccupied with the weight their decisions carry and the inevitable dissipation of their influence up and down the chain of command. This is the administrative version of "powerlessness."

An example of a middle-level administrator is this harried coordinator of a youth services group:

> When the adult group leaders who work under me disagree with my decisions, they think nothing of complaining to my superior, who as often as not overrules me. Last year I wanted to organize summer programs in the local communities—a week in each neighborhood. It was something we hadn't done before, and I thought it was worth trying out. Well, that got shot down because the organization placed top priority on maintaining its good old summer camps. Then one counselor assigned to a camp asked for time off to do some community work back in the city. Since we were now committed to having the camps, I refused permission because her absence would leave the camp inadequately staffed. She went to my superior, who countermanded my decision. Later the camp director protested. By this point I felt we might as well let the woman do what she wanted, but the camp director persuaded my superior to reverse herself and keep the woman in camp. From beginning to end I was overruled three times, and each time I found myself pleading with my superior (just for the sake of having some order and continuity) not to switch back to what I had wanted her to do the time before!

A head nurse reports:

> I'm supposed to be running the ward, but I can't make my decisions stick because I have no authority to discipline people. Whenever I try, the union challenges me. A three-day suspension I imposed was disallowed because a warning the person had received a year earlier hadn't been properly worded. So all I can do is to keep issuing warnings.

At the top management level we have the university administrator who has watched his fledgling human services training program grow from "a minor annoyance to a big nuisance" to the rest of the university:

The president and the trustees make flowery pronouncements about our having an "autonomous" program. What that means in practice is that I'm left without moorings. The administration gives me neither direction nor support, but "benign neglect." I can keep going the way I am as long as there are no complaints. It's uncomfortable having to make decisions without ever knowing whether I'll be able to bring the institution along with me. The best I can do is break even. If I'm right, fine; that's what I'm getting paid for. If I'm wrong, I hear about it right quick!

BAD OFFICE POLITICS

"Bad office politics" encompasses all the large and small problems people have in getting along with each other in situations where power depends on position. "Bureaucratic" issues come under this heading. A psychologist appointed to head a clinic treads softly in the presence of his predecessor, who remains at the clinic as a consultant. An affirmative action officer at a job-training center steels herself to exercise her authority to reverse discriminatory orders issued by her boss, the affable agency director, at the behest of his "buddies" in the community. A nurse resents having to "waste time disguising my decisions to look like they came from the administration, so that the administration, being able to claim credit for them, will more likely support them." A teacher bitterly recites the rules of the "tenure game" in the public school system:

> Tenure is conferred upon a person for breathing and for not physically harming or seducing any students. If I did those things for three years—oh, yes, and monitored the johns, maintained study hall, showed up 15 minutes early and stayed 15 minutes late, and generally conformed to the image of a "public servant" (that is, a lackey for the system)—I would be granted tenure.

A paraprofessional alcoholism counselor chafes at the restrictions he is placed under following an argument with the head counselor, while in an upstairs office the director of the treatment center weighs the likelihood of "petty harassment" from state officials if he challenges them on matters of policy. "They can't hurt me personally," he thinks, "but they can make sure I don't get everything I want on my next budget request—whatever the consequences for the people we're serving!"

There are several complaints that people typically have about large bureaucratic organizations. There is "status-quoism"—a seemingly relentless determination to keep clients, staff, and the institution just the way they are. There is what Sidney Simon calls "red-pencil mentality"—the habit of looking for reasons why something cannot be done instead of for ways of doing it. In a place where everyone is wary of institutional politics and afraid to take risks, it is easiest for all concerned to agree that nothing new should be attempted. When defeatism is universal, anyone who does want to get something done will need to maintain a high pitch of inner energy and determination.

A major source of disillusionment with institutions is the discrepancy between statement and practice. "They talk a good line about innovation," runs a typical observation, "but what do they really do?" Again, while it is usually front-line personnel who voice such criticisms, it is not hard to find a top manager who will say something like this:

> You should see the "statements of mission" and "guidelines" we have in our catalogues. Our original statement of purpose included community services that the legislature never appropriated a penny for. A revised statement went even further, but brought no additional funding. A couple of years ago there was a great ferment in our area. The college administration wrote up guidelines, duly enacted by the board of trustees, that mandated funding and full recognition of the program by the college. A visitor from outer space might expect to see some correlation between these directives and the actuality. But that's all the guidelines really do; they make the program look good to someone who's reading the catalogue.

Staff polarization is another aspect of organizational life that creates resentment and reduces the effectiveness of personnel. Partly on account of the structure of the institution, and partly on account of human contrariness, people form groups and develop competing interests based on labels that they learn to apply to themselves. An area in which polarization is especially evident is alcohol and drug addiction counseling, where exclients who are "recovering" or "drug-free" are considered to have a special expertise that rivals that of trained professionals. Within a treatment facility there may be considerable discrimination against exaddict counselors (as we saw in Roger F.'s story of the "clinical conference"), but there is also discrimination *in favor of* exaddicts, particularly in hiring. Thus a person who has obtained an associate's degree in order to work with addicts may come out of school into a "buyer's market" where those with a history of substance abuse are preferred. Polarization between professionals and paraprofessionals also creates what the director of one rehabilitation center lists as his Wild Card frustration: "Lack of cooperation among agencies." He cites the destructive competition for funds among institutions, as well as the territorial battles between groups such as Alcoholics Anonymous and medical or social work professionals. There has always been some resentment on the part of those who contribute volunteer service as fellow sufferers toward those who earn their living helping alcoholics. (This attitude has recently been evolving into one of greater cooperation.) The same sorts of jealousies and power struggles have been observed to occur when drug and alcohol counselors work together in the same agency, as the "goodies" vie with the "baddies" for funds and top-level jobs. Where these conflicts are intense, one needs to have the kind of poise shown by this psychiatric social worker at an alcohol detox unit:

> As supervisor of counseling I expect the staff to look at things from the same perspective I do. They don't, of course. Most of the counselors are recovering alcoholics who want to work spe-

cifically with addiction. The professionals, meanwhile, think in terms of people and their feelings. This split was a problem to me initially, but I have learned to bridge the gap by understanding alcoholics as what they are—people with universal feelings. As for *my* feelings, I've come to see that someone who gets angry at me for not being an alcoholic is just as likely to get angry with the next person for being one.

In every kind of helping agency, polarization occurs around academic credentials. Those who have them line up against those who do not. Note both the conscious and unconscious stress on the "degree" in these remarks by a prison administrator:

> The way the system is set up here, it is much harder for a non-degree person to get a promotion than for a degree person. This creates problems, as much as I would prefer otherwise. One gentleman I worked with—a counselor, a non-degree person, but an extremely good counselor (at least at that time—he had problems later)—had been acting director because of a vacancy in the position to which I subsequently was appointed. When I came in as director, he had to move down. Naturally this created some tension, since he and I had to work closely together.

The man who spoke these words is young, sensitive, and idealistic. Even so, he identifies his colleague by his non-degree status, which he then apologizes for with a hasty nod to the man's competence. Imagine if he had said, "a counselor I worked with —a black man, but an extremely good counselor" or "a woman, but an extremely good counselor." With all his fair-mindedness, he reveals a subtle prejudice, one that most of us unconsciously subscribe to. Before you are anything else, you are a "degree" person or a "non-degree" person.

People who do have degrees square off not only against those who do not have degrees, but against those who have different degrees. A case example is the rivalry between psychiatrists and psychologists, seen here through the eyes of the chief psychologist in a mental institution:

Psychiatric services in hospitals are run by medical people. Those in other disciplines are underutilized, to the detriment of patient services. Psychologists are used for group work and diagnostic testing, but in most cases not for individual therapy. "Managing" a case is left to the M.D., who often is not as well trained to handle it. Most of the psychologists in my service are frustrated because they feel they could contribute more. I agree; I'm frustrated, too. Their dissatisfaction causes me to have to deal with a high turnover rate. Even those who don't complain about having such limited responsibility gripe about the salary differential between them and the doctors, as well as about not being authorized to prescribe drugs.

Probably the most intense and widespread form of polarization is that which occurs across the lines of status and power in an agency or institution—between superiors and subordinates, between those with front-line responsibility and those with managerial responsibility. Status distinctions are the basis of a hierarchical organization. Occasionally a person's status is unclear, as in the "no man's land" inhabited by exaddict counselors who are promoted to a supervisory level without being accorded professional standing. It is a tossup whether being in such limbo is better or worse than having a clearly defined status (as most people do), which gives one both natural allies and natural enemies. Here, for example, is what individuals in a number of fields think of the people who run their programs:

1.   A psychologist who has worked in a number of clinical, academic, and institutional settings: "The administrators of the mental health facilities where I have worked (with the exception of the university) have been, on balance, destructive. They have done more to impair than facilitate services. The people who are selected—and who select themselves—for these positions tend to be those whose desire for control exceeds their knowledge, training, and capacities. Often they are psychiatrists who would be in private practice if they were any good."

2. A public school teacher: "I've been very disillusioned with the quality of the people in high administrative posts. Sometimes I wonder if they didn't get their degrees in Crackerjack boxes. There seems to be a total alienation between the students on the one hand and the superintendents, board members, and department chairmen on the other. The only people left who can reach the students, aside from other students, are teachers who are not yet in a position to control what the students learn."

3. A young middle-level administrator in a federal job-training program: "The people who administer social service programs tend to be bureaucrats, frustrated social workers who have been 'kicked upstairs' to try managing what they can't themselves do (nor can they manage, of course), people who can't make it in the private sector—*and* a growing number of people who are committed to the public sector and trained to handle its intricacies."

There is a lot of truth in these descriptions—sometimes, and from a particular point of view.

As an illustration of staff polarization and the conflicting points of view it creates, we can take a hospital psychiatric ward. Its hierarchy consists of three levels: mental health workers (or "technicians" or "assistants"), nurses, and psychiatrists. The real polarization, however, is between the "nursing staff" (consisting of nurses and mental health workers) and the doctors. Although nurses are differentiated from mental health workers in pay, responsibility, and professional status, the two groups tend to make common cause. As one nurse put it, "We're together on the front lines. The doctors can get away. They can walk off that floor and leave us to deal with the patients hour after hour. For us there's no escape." On the typical psychiatric ward, this perception of "being in the same boat" unites the nursing staff against the psychiatrists. Here are some of the common complaints voiced by nurses and mental health technicians, together with replies from a physician working in a similar facility. We see that the doctor has a few complaints of his own.

> *Technician:* "The psychiatrists are supposed to come to staff meetings and team meetings and take us on rounds. But all the 'supposed to's' don't become a reality. The psychiatrists are inconspicuous on the unit. They'll see a patient for 5 minutes and scribble down a progress note without briefing the staff. It's up to us to ask them about the treatment plan, and they're not too happy about being asked. Sometimes they'll be honest and say, 'You do your thing and we'll do ours,' which doesn't do much for the patient."
>
> *Doctor:* "In a state mental hospital an undermanned, inadequately trained, demoralized staff (the state doesn't always pay them on time) has the fantasy that psychiatrists can make everything okay. Psychiatrists can't give patients good jobs and people to love them; they can only tinker with what's there. The staff consists of 'psychiatric' nurses who don't have enough special training to live up to their name, along with mental health aides, some of whom are just learning the job and preparing to move on while others are stuck in dead-end jobs. Some of these people are 'institutionalized'; when they've been there for thirty years it gets hard to tell them apart from the patients. For these people the doctor is a convenient scapegoat. It's easier for them to blame the doctor for not giving a patient enough drugs to keep him from becoming violent than to blame themselves for not knowing how to enable the patient to express himself another way. Patients need a therapeutic milieu in which they can learn to control their behavior. Lacking a trained staff of sufficient size to create such a milieu, the psychiatrist is under pressure from frightened staff members (who don't want the responsibility of dealing with patients) to keep patients under control with excessively high doses of drugs. Sooner or later he succumbs to that pressure, or else the staff will keep using bureaucratic rules to make his life miserable. After a while he can't go on living with his conscience (or with the threat of malpractice suits), and he leaves to take another job."
>
> *Nurse:* "It's incredible that a head nurse with years of experience working with the same kinds of patients—in some cases

with the same patients—has no say over where a patient is put on the ward. We nurses know about ward administration; the residents don't. But they use us as data collectors while they make the decisions. The only power we have with the doctors is the power of persuasion. I've said to a resident, 'I've observed this patient for two years, and you've talked to her once. Now you're going to tell me how to handle her?' They just don't listen."

Doctor: "A psychiatric nurse who had been at that hospital for thirty years called me after I had admitted a patient with orders that he be given a certain number of units of insulin. She asked, 'Which kind of insulin should he get—40, 80, or 100 units per cc?' I replied, 'Any kind, as long as you give the right number of units. You just have to match the package with the syringe.' She knew this; she just didn't want to know. At first I tried to be as nice as I could about it, but she kept after me for 15 minutes. Finally she asked me if I was a 'real medical doctor.' I told her, 'I am, and a unit of insulin is a unit of insulin is a unit of insulin.' This was how she tried to put all the psychiatrists on the defensive—especially me, because I spoke to the patients, which threatened her control."

Technician: "The system is set up to give the psychiatric residents experience. We're the ones who are training the physicians —only don't ever let them hear you say so!"

Doctor: "Most people forget that the people you learn the most from, the people who really are training you, are the patients. The nursing staff does play a part in training residents. But this 'Who's training who?' game is just part of the hierarchical ethos: 'I'm training you, so you are below me, and that means you have to do what I want.' "

Nurse: "I feel like Cassandra, prophesying the future while no one listens. A patient was in seclusion with stage-three mania. For a week she was too crazy to eat or drink. She was dehydrated, but the doctor would not medicate her. We bugged him and bugged him: 'She'll die in that room if we don't give her anything.' The doctor said, 'I want to observe her. If I medicate for illness I'll never know what her diagnosis is.' What was the point of a diagnosis if she was dead? Finally I had to go to a meeting of the hospital administration and tell them that a woman who was being left untreated in the seclusion room was about to die. Within half an hour that woman was receiving medication. But the doctor wouldn't listen to me."

Doctor: "When I was an intern at a general hospital, it was with great trepidation (and frustration) that I left each service after my six-week rotation. While I was there, I tried to keep in mind that patients are human beings in pain. I tried to give patients what they needed—whether it was antibiotics, food, or a few kind words—without routinely bringing to bear the hospital's massive diagnostic apparatus. But as soon as I was gone, the hospital system fell back into place. Everybody covered themselves by doing exactly what everybody else would do—which was to test and test so that they could be 'sure' before they would act to relieve suffering. The tests, necessary or not, *created* suffering in the form of pain, stress, and infections."

Technician: "Psychiatrists are all the same. They're egotistical and unconcerned about the patients. What's frightening is that they're all alike, so there must be something in their background that makes them the way they are."

Doctor: "When I interned in a hospital emergency room, they kept a record of how many patients each intern saw. They told us when we saw 'too few' patients. That made us concentrate on doing things that appeared in the record book. Lab results appeared in the book; talking to patients didn't. Besides, it took more time to talk to patients than to send them to the lab. We began to get angry at patients who asked too many questions because they were taking up our precious time. Another control mechanism they used was to make us responsible for all the patients who were still in the emergency room when our duty hours ended. That way, if we had been working 'too slowly' all day, we might end up getting out of there at 3 a.m. Since we were all in the same boat, we'd all get angry at whoever was especially slow. The institution enforced its aims by means of peer pressure, which is more savage than hierarchical pressure.

"Meanwhile, patients were waiting 3 or 4 hours to be seen by a doctor. The hospital could have cut down the waiting time by adding two more doctors a day—a 5 percent addition to a 2-million-dollar budget. But the hospital didn't really want to cut down the waiting time. When the interns were put under pressure to make decisions quickly and were prevented from spending enough time with patients to satisfy themselves, they admitted more patients to the hospital, 'just to make sure,' rather than take responsibility for sending them home. Once admitted, the patients (or their insurers) could be hit for all kinds of costly tests and procedures that couldn't be done in the emergency room."

A similar exchange took place between another psychiatrist and a staff member:

> *Nurse:* "We have patients who regularly beat up staff members. At staff meetings we're told, 'Touch luck. You have to go in there and medicate him. So what if he sent two people home on a stretcher.' It doesn't do that patient any good to keep him in a place where we can't manage him. There he stays, though, as long as it's just us and not the doctors he's attacking. But just let him beat up a doctor, and they'll get him out of there right away."
>
> *Doctor:* "Front-line people assume that administrators know a lot more than they actually do. They don't realize how isolated the top people are from what's going on. If they don't bring their grievances to the attention of the administration, then their own lack of potency is partly responsible for the perpetuation of these injustices. They're dumping the responsibility on everyone but themselves."

What do we learn from these commentaries? We can draw several conclusions:

1. The "system" affects doctors in some of the same ways that it affects the nursing staff.
2. Doctors confirm some of the hardships alleged by the nursing staff.
3. Doctors, like nurses and aides, labor under some genuine difficulties.
4. Doctors, like nurses and aides, are very much influenced by their point of view and are capable of rationalizing their position.

A nurse gives this cynical overview of "bad office politics" in two types of helping institutions:

> In the hospital the doctors dump on the nurses, who dump on the patients and secretaries and orderlies, who dump on one another. It was the same way at the drug counseling center where I worked previously. Clients, staff, and administration

fought it out. When the administration won a battle, the staff took out their frustration on clients and on each other.

There is no use in underestimating the jealousies, the infighting, the undercutting of ambitions and reputations that goes on not only on the psychiatric unit, but in any kind of organization. Some people go into the helping professions with the idea that a facility dedicated to helping people will not be the scene of conflict and rivalry. In contrast, a government social services planner candidly reports, "There's conflict everywhere in life. I went into politics because at least there it's out in the open." "Politics" is one of the "givens" in any field. It might be better if it weren't there, but it is. There may be more or less of it, and people may be more or less sensitive to it. But everyone needs to accept it and deal with it realistically.

Chapter 7

THE GIVENS OF THE SYSTEM

If politics is one of the "givens" of the system, so is the system's seeming unresponsiveness to the needs of the client, of the individual worker, and of society—the very needs it has been set up to serve. The subordination of client services to administrative and political requirements, the lack of appreciative recognition of the helper's efforts on the part of supervisors and clients alike, the paper work that drains the energy of dedicated helpers, the failure of training programs to prepare trainees for the actual conditions of the job—all of these common complaints point to basic incongruities in the help-giving institution. These are the "givens." They are real sources of frustration. At the same time, they are the parameters within which all concerned must learn to work.

SYSTEM NOT RESPONSIVE TO CLIENTS' NEEDS

Arthur T. is an Army officer who counsels servicemen with emotional and behavioral problems. When asked to assess the impact of his work, Arthur speaks with studied correctness, but also with regret:

Some years ago the Army came to the conclusion that, in order to accomplish its mission, it had to have people—reliable, productive people. In order to keep people in the service and keep them happy, it would have to pay more attention to their needs. It would have to identify people who needed help with problem areas in their careers.

As a matter of policy, when a person gets into trouble, that person will be seen and assisted. To carry out this policy an enormous administrative apparatus has come into being. The client must be seen, so the client is seen. The paper work must then be completed to show that the client was seen. Everyone must know that the Army has met its requirements to the individual. Yes, the Army takes care of its own, but for its own sake.

I can tell when clients feel they are being run through the system to satisfy an administrative requirement. They appreciate what I'm doing, but too often they leave here feeling that they could do more to resolve the problem if they had more time with me. Sometimes that's too simple an answer, an excuse on their part. Other times I feel the same way they do. I see the needs of the individual and the needs of the Army, but I can't always reconcile them. At the end of a session I can always feel that I've met all the requirements of the Army. I can't always feel that I've met all the requirements of the individual.

To me it is painful. When I multiply my own pain, my own desire to help, by the number of counselors stationed all over the world, I wonder when somebody is going to say, "What are we doing here? We're wasting so much emotional energy trying to accomplish something that can't be accomplished the way we're doing it."

"Taking care of its own, for its own sake," the military—as perceived by those who give and receive human services within it—is the epitome of the self-serving bureaucratic institution. Are civilian help-giving agencies, seen through the same lenses, any different? Here is what Arthur's counterparts in a wide range of agencies have to say:

1.   A nurse running a ward in a busy metropolitan hospital: "The fiscal needs of the hospital corporation are met first, the patients' needs second. Management checks up on you all the time. At these evaluations

they give you a list of things that are wrong; they don't mention that the patients look healthy or happy."

2. A science teacher in a public high school: "Although tests and measurements are set up to carry out 'needs assessment,' the students themselves never form the basis of those data. It is always the assumptions and expectations of board members and administrators that determine the findings. The underlying, unspoken goal is for the system to perpetuate itself. The school isn't there for the students; the students are there for the school."

3. A counselor who works with prison inmates: "Sometimes I think (and it may be my imagination—I hope it is) that the system maintains itself to keep people employed. As for the inmates, 'Well, what the hell, they're only criminals anyway.' Agency politics creates a subsystem of competing interests that undermines the service that the institution was created to provide."

4. A project administrator in a community volunteer services program: "I've sat in on planning sessions where important people were designing programs to serve the community. None of these people had ever worked in the community; how could they know what the needs were? Five-year need assessments are being put together by people who have never talked to a client or directly supervised a counselor."

5. A psychiatric nurse in an urban drug clinic: "Drug treatment is a numbers game. You feel the pressure to keep up the census in order to get more funding. And what's the easiest way to do that? Methadone maintenance. It's a quick, inexpensive, high-volume treatment that keeps patients under control. They don't even try to determine what's the best dose for people. The priorities here are the same as they were at the university teaching hospital where I once worked,

where they kept hopelessly ill patients alive on respirators for research purposes."

6. The director of a regional center for alcoholism treatment: "Money is allocated not for what clients need, but for what politicians want. The largest allocation is for the least significant part of treatment—detox. We find ourselves in the position of having to design programs to qualify for funds that have all kinds of strings attached. It's 'ass-backwards,' as far as I'm concerned. It amounts to making people fit the mold. We should have funds allocated for alcoholism treatment, period, and then design the programs to meet people's needs."

If we are to believe these disgruntled remarks, there is a systematic institutional disregard for the needs of clients—for *people*—in favor of administrative requirements, financial pressures, and bureaucratic jockeying for power. Top-heavy hierarchies grind on like perpetual motion machines, justifying their existence with *pro forma* nods to the people they are supposed to serve. How true is this picture?

Half true. To the person on the front lines, bureaucracy works with agonizing slowness and indifference. Faceless administrators—referred to as "they" or "the people up there"—make decisions or non-decisions the consequences of which they will not directly face and therefore (according to the line staff) cannot understand. The great lumbering beast called "the system" moves toward a decision at its own leisurely pace. Meanwhile, funds are not made available, and people suffer.

On the other hand, there are not many top administrators who come to work in the morning gleefully rubbing their hands together and thinking, "Let's see how many people I can shortchange and swindle today." What they do say to themselves is more like this: "How can I look good today, or at least not look bad? How can I do a good job while protecting and advancing my own position?" This is what the front-line people are thinking, too. It is what everybody is thinking. It is one of the "givens" of the social, political, and economic system we live under.

When people say that their agency is not responsive to clients' needs, they mean that it is not responsive to the area of assistance in which they themselves are working and the needs they see first hand. Top managers, removed from the immediacy of the situation, see clients' needs differently, from a broader perspective, though not necessarily more accurately. What the counseling staff sees as an emergency will appear to the board of directors as a routine matter to be dealt with through normal administrative procedures. The staff may feel, for example, that a new paint job for the counseling center would give the morale of both clients and staff a crucial boost. Given the results they anticipate, they may consider the cost of paint and labor to be a bargain, and they may be right. The directors, though, have to weigh the costs and benefits of this proposed expenditure against others, such as developing training programs and hiring better-qualified personnel, whose effects may not be so immediately apparent to the staff. They also have to administer and fund other facilities besides the one in question.

The dispute goes on at all levels. The directors feel toward "the politicians" what the front-line staff feels toward them. General Douglas MacArthur resented the "desk soldiers" in Washington in the way that a drug rehabilitation counselor might resent agency officials who issue directives while remaining safely behind the battle lines. Neither side is completely right or completely wrong. But the discontent is undeniably there. It is a fact that must be kept in mind in understanding Burn-out, whether in oneself or in one's subordinates.

NOT APPRECIATED BY SUPERVISOR

The unresponsiveness of the "system" toward the people working in it is experienced as a lack of appreciation. A person who is not given responsibility, is not consulted about decisions, and is generally overlooked by the bureaucratic "system" will certainly feel unappreciated by his or her supervisor and by the organization as a whole. On the polarized psychiatric ward that we visited, staff members give and receive what they feel is honest feedback, positive and negative, among their peers. This feedback includes support, praise, and encouragement as well as correction. From their superiors, however, they hear only criticism. The administrator whose positive accomplishments go unnoticed while his errors are thrown back in his face ("the best I can do is break even by having things run smoothly," he laments) is suffering the effects of lack of appreciation by the higher-ups as well as "no support for important decisions."

A drug counselor, formerly a drug user himself, who is treated as a "quasi-patient" gets into frequent conflicts with his supervisor over his narrowly defined responsibilities. Acting out his assigned role as a disabled, irresponsible person, he gets drunk while on duty and goes off to have an affair with a woman client, leaving the facility unattended. The next day he receives an official telegram instructing him never again to set foot on state property. He is bitter at the lack of acknowledgment of all that he had previously contributed to the treatment program. In his case the feeling of not being appreciated by his employers has come into play twice—first when he was not accorded sufficient status and responsibility all along, and then when the state peremptorily washed its hands of him.

But the most poignant account of what it means to beat one's head against the wall of managerial indifference (or even hostility) comes from an ex-schoolteacher:

> None of us can grow, professionally or otherwise, without positive reinforcement. Try and get some. A teacher is observed twice a year, in the spring and fall, when the superintendent calls in the teacher ratings. The principal, who has no knowledge of the teacher or the subject, then comes into the classroom and evaluates things that are irrelevant to the learning process. I was told—and it still angers me—that I did not keep enough sharp pencils on my desk. It didn't matter that I had revised the school's American literature program to cover the years since 1936 (which apparently was when the program had last been

revised). It didn't matter that I had started the district's first successful theater program with no funding and no assistance. But let there be a dime jammed into the coke machine after rehearsal, and you can be sure I was held responsible.

NOT APPRECIATED BY CLIENTS

Appreciation from clients is what enables one to go on in the face of lack of institutional support. One can take the hassles one gets from the principal and superintendent when one is revered by one's students. When they, too, are unappreciative, it calls into question one's whole purpose in being there. Helping people is what it's all about. What happens when they don't see themselves as being helped?

Issues of client relations and client satisfaction particularly concern front-line workers who spend their time directly with clients. These individuals, who are not primarily occupied with exerting bureaucratic control, do not have the satisfactions or the frustrations that come from seeing the larger organizational picture. Many have not had the professional training that would help them detach themselves from immediate results— including expressions of gratitude from cooperative clients—as the main justification of their work.

Lack of appreciation occurs most commonly with clients who do not want help in the first place. Clients who deny that they have a problem at all are not likely to thank anyone for trying to help them. Heroin addicts often are quite content to go on living as they have been; alcoholics, of course, are notorious deniers. A welfare caseworker describes the attitude of many of the people she works with:

> It isn't the way you learn in school or read about in books. In order to change their behavior, people have to be willing to work very hard. Many of the people a public welfare agency gets involved with not only have little awareness of their problems, but also have little interest in improving their situation. They don't want to get to the roots of things and make significant

changes. They just want a band-aid, some temporary alleviation of the pain.

A social worker who investigates reports of child abuse finds herself, understandably, almost always working in a hostile environment:

> When I go to someone's home I'm coming into a charged situation. The family doesn't want me there. They spend a lot of time denying my reason for being there and claiming that things are just great. What can you do for a family like that?

The clients who are least appreciative are the ones who are coerced into the helping situation. Counselors in the military services have the dispiriting task of greeting people who, for whatever reason (alcoholism, drug use, absenteeism, behavior problems), have been *ordered* to report for counseling. Some of these clients feel doubly coerced, having been drafted into the service in the first place. Among the coerced clients in civilian life are those who are sentenced to prison, committed to a mental institution, placed on probation, or referred by a court for treatment in lieu of incarceration (treatment thus becoming incarceration). There are also many who feel that they have been pressured into a counseling situation by their families or employers. It is not surprising that counselors who face such unwilling clients meet with a great deal of denial and hostility. To the coerced client, a "helper" is an authority in sheep's clothing. To the helper, it is frustrating to have to act in a custodial capacity. "I feel like a cop, keeping tabs on people for the courts," says a young employee of a state-run alcoholism treatment center.

At the other extreme, clients who *do* want to be helped tend to ask for more than the helper can give. According to an experienced social worker, "Each person you see thinks he or she is the only one you're serving. People don't understand volume. They don't understand low staffing, budget limits, and all the other constraints on what you can do. You have to explain to them what you're up against." This basic difference in perspective is inherent in the helping relationship, especially in institutional contexts. Clients see only their own situation, their own needs, their own relationship with the helper. The helper sees that time, money, and services have to be apportioned among many clients. These are the "facts of life" that have to be communicated to clients, who do not always get the message.

It is frustrating to put out for people only to have one's efforts go unappreciated—to have people turn away in indifference or clamor for more. The helper has to have some way of coming to terms with the stresses and disappointments of dealing with unappreciative clients. One alcoholism counselor says, "When I feel myself getting wound up I stop and ask myself how many years and how many people it took to bring *me* around. I say to myself, 'I guess *you* got cured the first time they put you in a hospital.'" One of his colleagues deals with the question of appreciation by turning it on its head. "I've found that the ones who *say* I've saved them are the ones I haven't really helped," he reports. "The ones who say, 'You haven't done a goddamn thing for me,' are the ones I *have* helped—by teaching them to do it themselves."

TOO MUCH PAPER WORK

A university professor who acts as assistant to the department chairman is asked by the administration to compile a record of student performance over the past fifteen years. To him this information has little value for monitoring and improving the current performance of students. It is simply a job he must do to meet the needs of his supervisors. Since he is not offered any secretarial assistance in handling this additional work load, he has less time to spend with students during office hours. "My time is all I have to give," he says. "When it is allocated by people who are far removed from the day-to-day work of teaching, it tends to be misused. After a while it seems that I'm being directed into those activities that are least consequential in terms of achieving the goals of a university."

Those who gripe about "bureaucracy" are talking not only about a hierarchical power structure, but also about the official record-keeping requirements that are known as "paper work." Paper work is frustrating because it takes people away from the job they want to do. A counselor who is filling out forms is at that moment not serving people, but rather is serving the organization. Thus, paper work is often cited as evidence that "the system is not responsive to clients' needs." Paper work makes the front-line worker an administrator and takes the administrator farther away from front-line work. As one counselor put it, "I'm no clerk! This wasn't what I was hired to do."

The helping professions, operating to a great extent under government auspices (Federal, state, and local), are compelled to put up with the elaborate record keeping that cautious government bureaucracies insist upon. No organization more assiduously "covers itself" with official paper than that great plodding beast, the military. A counselor in one of the services gives this graphic estimate of the drain on his time: "I'd say I spend an hour and a half on the session with the client and an extra hour on the paper work. From the client's standpoint this time could better be used for additional counseling." Although the military may be an extreme example, "helpers" who spend 40% of their work time on paper work can be found wherever the need for professional or institutional self-justification (as in protecting against malpractice claims or accounting for methadone dosages or the whereabouts of parolees) creates a need for documentation. Schools, universities, hospitals, prisons, and military services are accountable to a nervous populace for the money they spend, the people they take responsibility for, and the principles they are charged to uphold. Record keeping is the means by which these institutions account for themselves. Its cost, ironically, is a reduction of the very effectiveness an organization would want to document.

Frustration with administrative record keeping is expressed in remarks like "Paper work deals with what's already been accomplished" and "You spend so much time writing down what you have done and what you're going to do that you don't have time to do anything." Paper work involves either review (past) or planning (future). Although these functions may be necessary for the organization, individuals who go into the helping professions desire to live and work in the present. The immediacy of person-to-person contact is what attracts people to the field. Paper work undermines this sense of immediacy and puts a distance between the person serving and the person served.

Although paper work claims the energies of personnel at all levels, its effects are increasingly felt as a person ascends the organizational ladder. The less training and responsibility one has, the less one is burdened with paper work. People who have "risen from the ranks" have found that each promotion brings with it an increased load of paper work. Managers of large organizations (hospitals, drug clinics, university departments) discover that paper work grows in proportion to the complexity of the organization and the number of clients it serves.

For those who despair of getting out from under the burden of paper work, a "solution" to the problem is offered by a self-proclaimed "Jekyll–Hyde" with a graduate degree who counsels drug abusers by day and abuses drugs herself by night. "Paper work?" she says. "Oh, that. I just don't do it." Those for whom that solution is not available can only go on living and working with the problem.

Not Sufficiently Trained for Job

Very few people say that they are adequately trained for their jobs. Those who do are often those who see their job descriptions as being very limited: "What training do you need to be a counselor in *this* godforsaken place?" Otherwise, the insecurities that afflict nearly everyone who tries to cope with complex human problems make it only natural to wish that one had been better prepared.

Insufficient training is understandably a major concern of those who do not have a background in human services skills —i.e., paraprofessionals with or without a college education. Without classroom instruction and supervised field experience in social work, psychology, or a related discipline, many enthusiastic A.A. members and Daytop alumni have found it hard to cope with the dynamics of the helping relationship. What is perhaps more surprising is that this preoccupation does not abate at higher levels of education and responsibility. It is not just paraprofessionals who worry about the adequacy of their training. The higher one rises, the more new areas of competence one has to be concerned about mastering.

This is especially true in the case of administrative skills. Most human services administrators were not trained to be administrators because they never intended to *become* administrators. Once out in the field, however, they rose from frontline, direct-service positions to supervisory posts. The head nurse was at one time a bedside nurse; the director of a clinic began as a practicing psychologist; today's department head was yesterday's classroom teacher. Their complaint (the most frequently voiced complaint under this heading) is that their original career training did not prepare them to handle an administrative job, or even the administrative aspects (paper work, for example) of a regular job in the human services. "My training prepared me pretty well for working with the inmates," says a counselor in the correctional system, "but not for negotiating the intricacies of departmental politics. That's a very different type of sociology." A psychiatrist reports, "Clinically, of course, my training was useful, but not when it came to office management, bookkeeping, and writing proposals for grants." A professor who became first a department head and then the dean of a school within the university wonders what a training program for college administrators would be like:

> It would have to teach people how to develop organizational

objectives and relate them to existing or potential resources. I was not exposed to anything of this sort in my training as an educator. I suppose I would have had to go to business school to get that.

If some people are dissatisfied because their training was oriented more toward practice than administration, others have the opposite complaint. A schoolteacher echoes many in her profession when she says, "I consider myself overtrained. My training was too academic, too theoretical, not directed sufficiently toward working with people." A drug rehabilitation counselor currently working toward an M.S.W. degree describes himself as "doing it mostly for career advancement. I would not say I'm learning much about the job. Mostly it's paper work and administration."

The fact that people complain about having had either too much or too little administrative training, too much or too little practical training, suggests the near impossibility of one's finding a perfect match between one's professional education and later experience on the job. It is just too hard to predict what one is going to face on the job, both over the long haul and on any given day. An alcoholism counselor with 12-step A.A. experience feels at a disadvantage because he does not understand "social process" as a trained social worker does. A trained social worker with a working knowledge of psychiatric diagnosis is at a loss to help alcoholics and their families because she has not studied alcoholism or family counseling. There are always specific tasks, unexpected problems, new variations for which one is not sufficiently trained.

A school psychologist gets to the heart of the matter with this observation: "To understand the theory you have to have the direct experience first. You have to get to know how changeable people really are." A clinical psychologist elaborates:

> Certainly I got a lot out of my training, but when it came to developing my own style and approach, I could only do that through an apprenticeship. You can't learn a helping profession

in the abstract. In my case, at any rate, the "school of hard knocks" proved more valuable than the school where I took my Ph.D.

According to this psychologist, the quality of one's work as a therapist depends less on one's formal training than on personal traits such as openness, attentiveness, and willingness to work. Her view is in line with numerous studies that show therapeutic effectiveness to be unrelated to the particular school or discipline in which the therapist has been trained.[1] It is on the basis of this research that Sidney Wolf[2] lists ten character traits of a good counselor: empathy, respect, genuineness, concreteness, confrontation, self-disclosure, immediacy, warmth, potency and self-actualization. Training cannot give a person these traits, but a good training program enhances them.

A family services caseworker comments:

> In this field you have to make life-or-death decisions, such as whether a parent gets to keep custody of a child. Who is ever prepared to make such decisions? No amount of training can confer upon you the wisdom of Solomon. There's always an element of uncertainty that you have to deal with on your own.

A large element of uncertainty attends any situation involving human feelings and behavior. Perhaps the most useful thing a training program can do, besides supplying certain essential skills, is to make the trainee aware of that uncertainty. There is a paradox here. On the one hand, obtaining further training in the field is one of the best ways to combat frustration and increase one's effectiveness as a helper. As we shall see in Chapter 11, it can be a crucial intervention. On the other hand, no one ever is "sufficiently trained for the job." There will always be more skills to learn, and there will always be dilemmas that baffle even those skills. Everyone complains about not having enough training—because no one can have enough. Perhaps, then, the most apt response to this item on the planning board comes from a health planner in a government agency who quipped, "If I'm not sufficiently trained, it's my fault."

Chapter 8

FRUSTRATIONS, REACTIONS, AND CONSEQUENCES

Along with the sources of frustration, it is important to understand how frustration compromises services to clients, how it affects helpers themselves, and some of the ways in which individuals can and do react to it. This chapter will take up these questions after a brief look at some important frustrations that are not included in the 12-point planning board exercise.

"Wild Card" Frustrations

The "Wild Card" on the planning board—the sheet left blank for the 12th frustration—has been very useful in enabling people to bring out, in their own words, issues that matter to them. Issues that come up repeatedly can then be incorporated into the planning board when applicable—e.g., when the person doing the exercise is a woman, an administrator, or whatever. Here, briefly, are some of the most commonly cited frustrations, the ones people talk about of their own accord.

Sexism

Tales of sexism echo from one corner of the human services to another. A psychiatric nurse in a methadone clinic observes that male counselors are indifferent when women addicts show clear evidence of having been beaten, and that no one seems to care how a given dose of methadone may affect a pregnant woman. A city school board decorously fills its "assistant principal" slots with women, each of whom will be working under a male principal. An impatient functionary on a hospital floor looks right past a white-coated woman doctor and asks, "Where's the doctor?" A nurse who brings the needs of a male patient to the attention of her supervisor is made the object of sexual innuendos. The same nurse notices that female nurses show a consistent preference for male patients, whom they regard as less demanding and easier to take care of than women.

Sexism compounds the inequalities of position and power that exist throughout the helping professions (as they do everywhere). The woman social worker who must accede to the wishes of highly paid judges and attorneys cannot help but see that most of them are men. The same goes for the teacher whose attempts at innovation are frustrated by complacent principals and school superintendents. On those psychiatric wards (and other hospital settings) that sometimes seem like armed camps, polarization along lines of professional authority is reinforced by sexual polarization, since most of the doctors and administrators are men, most of the nurses women. (The mental health workers, though, who are lowest on the totem pole, are as often men as women.) In such situations it can be difficult to disentangle sexual resentments from hierarchical ones. In the following account by a counseling supervisor in a drug treatment center for female adolescents, to what extent is the abuse of power an expression of sexism, and to what extent is it simply bureaucratic?

While our staff is with one exception all female, the director (and I've been here through four directors) is male. I'd like to see some more men in this all-female agency, and I'd also like to see a woman director as a positive model for the girls in treatment here. I resent the lack of public recognition given to the counselors, who spend all their time working with the girls. When the board of trustees comes around to inspect, when we have an open house for people in the community, when people from other agencies come to see what we're doing, it's the director who shows them around. We could speak for the agency as well as he can, but he's the one who gets the credit.

It would seem that the director is just assuming the normal prerogatives of his office, unjust as these may be. But there clearly are sexist overtones to the situation. The director may feel that he can get away with these repeated slights more readily with female staff members than with males. The inequity is certainly *felt* as gender-based by the aggrieved counselors, which makes that aspect of it a real part of their experience. And the structure of the institution, whereby one man holds a position of authority over many women, is sexist to begin with.

Sometimes the sexual issue is easily separable from the hierarchical. A woman family relations officer reports that lawyers treat her differently from her male counterparts:

The court system traditionally has been staffed by males at every level. In recent years this has begun to change, but most of the lawyers I deal with still are men. They know that a family relations officer's job is simply to study the situation and advise the court about what's going on. But with female family relations officers they don't respect those limits. They think they can get us to do their job for them. They don't want to sit and listen to a divorced lady with all her problems. They think that because I'm a woman they can get me to listen and then tell them what should be done. They want to use me as a labor-saving device to save them some of their precious time. They wouldn't try that with a male family relations officer.

Sexism affects clients, helpers, and administrators alike. A public school teacher gives this account of how, in her view, sexism pervades the school system:

> First, of course, there is the disproportionate number of women faculty members, which results from sex role stereotyping and "feminine programming." But mainly I want to talk about the imposition of stereotypes on students and teachers.
>
> Most public schools are predicated on the idea of perpetuating well-defined sex roles in the students. Teachers are expected to reward "masculine" behavior in boys, "feminine" behavior in girls. Androgynous behavior is frowned upon, and the polarity between the sexes is intensified. Young men who write poems instead of going out for sports are jeered—not by their peers, mind you, but in the faculty room. Young women who do go out for sports are subjected to condescension and name calling.
>
> The same is true for the faculty, who are, after all, considered "models" for the students. Women teachers are expected to act like "ladies," not women. A woman who is assertive or who works for change politically gets a negative response. Catcalls and sexual games are used to undermine the efficacy of women. Men faculty members are under tremendous pressure to prove their masculinity. A young male English teacher who understands metaphors but is not of rippling build can expect to hear sneering remarks at social gatherings.

Pressure to conform to sexual roles is internalized as a question of how one should behave and, ultimately, what one should be. Another woman schoolteacher remarks, "From what I can see, if women don't get many promotions, it's their own fault. I haven't met many dynamic women in the school system." But a woman who *is* dynamic soon finds that she is threatening to men both on and off the job. A psychiatric social worker describes the board of directors of her clinic as "bowling buddies" who resent the encroachments of a forceful professional woman. Women who put themselves "out on a limb" by being openly ambitious and upwardly mobile face similar reactions from male supervisors, fellow staff members, clients, and prospective husbands and lovers. A clinical psychologist confesses that she delayed getting her doctorate for a few years so as to avoid confronting the consequences of her achieved position. She wonders "how authoritative I can be as a therapist and still remain feminine in my personal life. Nothing is more challenging to many men than a woman psychologist—someone who they fear can see through them."

The institutionalized manifestations of sexism, although damaging to both sexes, almost always place women at a disadvantage when it comes to power. Sometimes, though, the sheer number of women working in a human services agency can reverse the balance. A psychiatric technician describes the sensation of being one of only two men on his unit as "sort of weird. The women form a close-knit group. I can't really joke around with them, so that leaves me one person with whom I can enjoy any kind of camaraderie." Disproportionate numbers, together with the absence of men in key posts, occasionally leave women in a position of real power. In one state hospital alcoholism program the doctors are young transients who, unlike the psychiatric residents we have observed, take a "hands-off" attitude toward what happens on the unit. As a result, the nurses and social workers run the program. In the accounts given by these women not only the issue of sexism, but those of powerlessness and bureaucratic conflict as well are notably absent. There is no hint of the hierarchical polarization that is almost universally present in hospital settings. Instead, there is "good communication," "good staff support," and "decision making by the group as a team." Professionals and paraprofessionals work together harmoniously—apparently because both groups are almost entirely composed of women.

Administrative Dilemmas

Although the concept of Burn-out originated with front-line staff, virtually every frustration one could name applies to administrators as well. In all areas we have discussed—particularly "no support for important decisions," "bad office politics," "too much paper work," and "not sufficiently trained for job"—we have seen middle and top managers, caught in the crossfire of bureaucratic decisions and non-decisions, going through their own varieties of frustration.

A psychiatrist who has administered state and federal addiction treatment programs as well as university training programs finds "more satisfaction *and* more frustration in management, where power struggles are a way of life. The stakes there are higher all around." As an administrator one has to be concerned with more than just one's own perspective on the agency and the people it serves. One must be able to see and (one hopes) reconcile a number of different perspectives on different sides of the issue—a skill which, like the traits of a good counselor, not everyone has. It is as if one is no longer just an individual doing a single job. Rather, one wears one hat for clients, one hat for subordinates, one hat for superiors, and one hat for the public (plus other hats as well, as for one's family or fellow A.A. members). Sometimes the administrator must change from one hat to another on very short notice—say, while running from one meeting to the next. A middle manager must learn to allocate authority and give subordinates the latitude to make wrong as well as right decisions—a relinquishing of immediate control that many find uncomfortable. (The alternative, which is to do everything oneself, is self-destructive and ultimately impossible.) A top manager faces the same political and public relations problems as in the private sector, along with the added travails of relatively low pay and a suspicious public constituency. Administrators at all levels are responsible for allocating scarce funds and dealing with the disappointments that inevitably result. Top managers have the additional problems of (for instance) having to plan programs before government funds have been budgeted and having to fund a growing organization on a stable appropriation.

Many administrators are in much the same position as the front-line worker who must explain to each client that he or she is not the only client the agency serves. When a social worker who has taken on supervisory responsibilities speaks of "staff members being at my jugular vein all day long," we seem to be back in the world of the paraprofessional drug counselor fighting off the clients who come in off the street seeking attention. A psychologist who teaches and runs a clinic at a university sums up the problem with his Wild Card selection: "too many demands by too many people." The pressures he faces come from students, private patients, clinic patients, clinic administrators, departmental colleagues, and so forth. "Each group wants me to be totally involved with its own sphere of activity, as if that were the only job I had." This man views all of his work—research, teaching, practice—as expressions of an integral viewpoint that he brings to the field. In practice, though, he receives constant reminders of the bureaucratic boundaries that separate one segment of his work from another. At times they are even in conflict, as when the clinic directors fail to see the relevance of his academic research.

The administrator often must accept what seems a sacrifice of personal integrity to do a near-impossible yet essential job. "I have to be a politician," says the director of an agency that coordinates alcoholism treatment services for several localities. "I'll be shaving off my goatee in the fall, because when I go to the community for support, I have to present myself in a way that's acceptable to them. I'll make that sacrifice for the people I'm trying to help." The head of a large government welfare planning agency describes her isolation as a manager in these terms:

> I've always avoided making friends in the agency or forming bureaucratic alliances in the staff office. I don't ever want to be in the position of having to decide against a friend. When it comes to letting someone go as part of a reorganization, I have to consider the well-being of the hundreds of clients we deal with annually, not the feelings of (or my own feelings toward) one staff member. To do this job you have to have a steel core inside you and steel walls around you, and sometimes you have to clang the gates shut.

It does not take a very long tour of duty in a highly visible managerial role before one develops a certain caution, a wariness of direct expression, a tendency to check oneself and the situation before articulating feelings or stating an opinion. Not surprisingly, it is difficult to find administrators who are willing to be interviewed for a book such as this one.

There is, however, at least one consolation for the person who wears many hats and is accountable to several constituencies. In the words of the psychologist who combines teaching and research with his clinic directorship, "At any given moment it's unlikely that things will be going badly on all fronts."

Bad Personal Image

Virtually everyone wants to be respected for the work one does. Unfortunately, the helping professions are not always prestigious occupations. The image of the schoolteacher in America, for example, is a split one. As one teacher puts it, "To the general population you represent the height of respectability. But educated people will denigrate you."

In cases where popular prejudice against the client (the alcoholic, the prison inmate, etc.) rubs off on the helper, one may be saddled with a negative image as well as with considerable popular misunderstanding of one's work. This also occurs commonly with nurses, who are seen as having an unclean sort of intimacy with ill patients. Overworked nurses cite the added frustration of having people ask them how they can do something so "gross." Here is a typical complaint:

> In nursing school, in social situations, and especially in the hospital there are unpleasant connotations attached to a woman being a nurse. Nurses are made the butt of jokes because of all the things they see. Doctors think they can say anything they want to a nurse. At parties people tell off-color jokes and expect me not to be offended. But the feeling of caring for someone who is ill, man or woman, is completely different from sexual feeling. The fact that I handle all parts of the body in the hospital doesn't

mean that I want to be "grossed out" in my personal life. I may
take care of men as a nurse, but that doesn't make me any less
of a lady.

The problem apparently is specific to female nurses. No one, it
seems, is bothered by the equally "gross" things male doctors
have to do. Whether this prejudice extends to female doctors
and to male nurses would make a useful inquiry.

Lack of Community Awareness and Support

Here the unfavorable public image applies not to the individual helper, but to a whole program. People who believe that
they are making it by virtue of their own hard work (and this
is the view most people have of themselves) do not like the idea
of supporting those who are unable or unwilling to do likewise.
They would just as soon not be exposed—or have their children
exposed—to "those people." This is why towns pass zoning
regulations to keep out certain facilities. This is why, when a
city-run drug program set up community clinics in Spanish-
speaking and Chinese-speaking neighborhoods, nearby mer-
chants blamed all neighborhood crimes on the addicts who
came to the clinics. This is why, as we have seen, the director
of an alcoholism treatment program "shaves his goatee in the
fall" before asking unsympathetic community leaders for funds
to set up a half-way house in their backyard. Each type of
agency maneuvers for its place in the sun in a political and
economic climate that currently is unfavorable for all.

The problems of dealing with obstructionist attitudes in
the community are graphically depicted by an official of a regional job-training agency who has tried to set up affirmative
action programs with the help of local mayors and town coun-
cils. "They'll listen," she reports, "but they won't let me *do*
anything. They all seem to be feeling what one woman council-
lor told me outright: 'Nobody ever helped *me.*' It's as if, having
made it themselves, they want to close the door behind them."

She expands on this point with an anecdote that typifies her (and her agency's) equivocal relationships with local politics and politicians:

> The clerk of one town employs two clients of ours who haven't worked out very well. I agree that we shouldn't have referred them, but it's also the case that on several occasions we have advised the town clerk to discipline them. Our exchanges with her have been like a broken record. "Why did you send them to me?" she asks. "Why did you hire them?" we reply. The answer —which we won't say to her any more than she'll say to us— is that they are town residents and voters. Hiring gets votes; firing loses votes. That's why she hires but expects us to fire.

When community leaders and media *do* put some stock in the helping professions, it is usually in the belief that a quick, decisive intervention will change long-standing behaviors and wipe out years of disadvantage and disability. Does that sound familiar? It is the same unrealistic expectation that people working in the helping fields have when they are just starting out. If the enthusiastic novice in the field is impatient, so is the "man on the street" who has had no experience whatsoever with the frustrations of the helper. And just as the individual helper burns out when grand expectations are disappointed, so public officials and taxpayers go through their own cycle of disillusionment. Community sentiment alternates between over-optimistic boosting and sullen disenchantment.

Disappointment with Peers

Along with all the problems one may have with supervisors, clients, and the community, it is also frustrating when one's fellow workers do not measure up to one's own image of idealism and dedication. Here are a few typical cases:

1.   A psychiatric technician: "I expected to learn more than I have on the job, and I expected the people I'm

working with to care more about learning than they actually do."

2. A nurse: "My 'Clara Barton' image of nursing was dimmed when I took my first hospital job after nursing school. Most of the other nurses were completely wrapped up in being at such a prestigious hospital, and I found them pretty dull. All they seemed to care about was meeting doctors."

3. A schoolteacher: "Most of the teachers I've known are chronic bitchers who put on weight over the years and complain about their aches and pains. My number one frustration is that my colleagues are unwilling or unable to think, either about the subject matter or about themselves and other people. There's no sense of growth, of change. I want to interact and share with people on the job, not bitch bitch bitch."

These people are concerned with something more than the lack of inspiring models and stimulating companions. In their descriptions of apathetic colleagues they see reflected images of what they themselves might become. It is as if they are telling themselves, "Watch out. This is what *you'll* be like in 10 or 20 years—if you don't fight it!"

EFFECTS ON CLIENT SERVICES

The effects of frustration—and of stagnation as well—on the quality of services rendered to clients have been all too evident throughout this discussion. Implicit and explicit in the accounts of overwork, inadequate funding, staff polarization, bureaucratic sluggishness, peer pressure to conform to a low performance standard, and other sources of discouragement and demoralization among staff members is the almost inevitable conclusion that the client ends up with the wrong end of the stick. Occasionally the cycle is broken through an act of will.

The young, idealistic assistant director of a community services agency was locked in an adversary relationship with the director, a somewhat complacent older man primarily concerned with protecting his good relationships with local businessmen and politicians. When asked whether this managerial conflict compromised her services to clients, the assistant director replied, "I don't let it affect my clients. If it does, then it's my fault." Few people, however, are capable of such consistent determination or assumption of responsibility. Besides, the structure of any institution larger than a storefront prevents any one individual, however determined, from being able to control the consequences of high-level decisions and bureaucratic conflicts.

Illustrations of clients caught in the crossfire of agency battles and of stagnation and frustration among helpers are not hard to find:

1. A prison guard: "A lot of the old-line staff, the guards who had been there for years, were quite embittered, and they would take it out on the inmates. Male guards, especially, would bait and insult women inmates. Even the female staff could be callous in denying requests that meant a lot to the inmates. They would say things like, 'Oh, don't bother with that. She's asked 15 people for that already.' "

2. A psychiatric nurse at a drug clinic: "Methadone was dispensed in the mornings, and the clients came in for counseling in the afternoons. The trouble was that the counselors, between being burned out from the heavy case load and being kept busy filling out forms for the FDA and NIDA, weren't able to do much counseling. They felt so inadequate to handle all the demands on them that they started avoiding clients and even not showing up for work. I saw clients coming in every day and asking, 'Where's my counselor?' "

3. A correctional counselor: "I worked closely with a

counselor who was not an educated professional, and his approach naturally was different from mine. We tried to cooperate, but there was a certain subtle competition between us. When it came to taking a client to a job interview, for example, we would discuss in advance how we would handle the company's personnel department. He had his way of doing it, and I had mine. Both of us were too stubborn to yield very much. I'm sure that had an effect on the outcomes of some of our clients' interviews."

Catherine Y., a counselor who lived and worked in the pressure cooker of a residential center for adolescent delinquent girls, tells how the *feelings* of frustration—the edginess, the irritability, the exhaustion—are transmitted from helper to client:

After going without sufficient rest for months I finally became too run-down to stay motivated. If a girl wanted to talk to me when I was tired, I couldn't stay alert enough to make the conversation therapeutic for her. In groups I couldn't stay on top of the group dynamics—who was participating, who was paying attention. Sometimes I would throw up my hands and say (to myself, of course), "I can't give any more right now. I just don't care."

I built up resentments against the director and the trustees. There were moments when I resented the girls because they got so much attention while no one seemed to care about *my* feelings. My resentment came out not in my denying them anything they needed, but in my being short-tempered with them for no good reason. If they did one little thing, I'd blow up. Once when I walked into the administrative office I found a girl who wasn't permitted to be there talking to one of the staff. Without any explanation I ordered her out of the office. That wasn't my normal way of acting, but by then things were building up inside me.

There was so much tension there that counselors were always going to other counselors to talk about their own upsets. Whole days were spent taking care of the counselors' problems instead of the residents'.

This is the completion of the contagion cycle of Burn-out. Frustration in the helping professions originates in part in bureaucratic difficulties, in part in client unresponsiveness, and in part in the intractability of certain human problems. It spreads among staff members in the form of indifference, cynicism, or griping. Clients pick up the prevailing attitudes from the staff, and their own morale suffers. As clients regress or fail to progress, staff frustration deepens. And so the cycle begins all over again.

The Symptoms of Frustration

A recovering alcoholic or addict who meets with frustration as a counselor may revert to destructive behavior. Someone who comes into the field without having a history of substance abuse or criminality does not have the option of acting out in that manner. Still, as the testimony of the counselor from the delinquent girls' home clearly shows, there are other ways of acting out, such as losing one's temper at clients. Catherine's story, together with the words she uses to tell it ("run-down," "tired," "tension"), reveals some of the physical, emotional, and behavioral manifestations of frustration. A head nurse in a nursing home tells what happens to her when the frustration builds up: "I get tension headaches; I smoke a lot; I'm impatient with my kids." Those are the three main areas in which frustration manifests itself for the individual worker: psychosomatic illness; unhealthful indulgence in food and drugs such as nicotine, caffeine, or alcohol; and damage to personal and family relationships (something we saw a lot of in previous chapters).

A mental health aide who himself complains of headaches and fatigue observes "everyone on the unit" coming down with low-grade fevers and chronic running noses. The director of an alcoholism clinic wakes up most mornings an hour too early, his heart pounding. A psychologist in private practice goes home "drained" from the intense concentration of therapy sessions. A nursing supervisor who celebrated her promotion by developing a stomach ulcer reports, "Now when I drink I get drunk." A young schoolteacher looks askance as her colleagues "put on weight over the years and complain about their aches and pains." Another teacher, her aspiration to excellence thwarted at every turn, goes through bouts of depression and anxiety punctuated by headaches, indigestion, and bronchitis:

> I was nervous, couldn't concentrate. My coping mechanisms, such as exercise, became less and less effective. The disappointment of my hopes was driving me to a nervous collapse. In my last two years of teaching I suffered a crisis of confidence where I was afraid to do anything. After I left teaching I stayed in limbo for two years. My world had caved in.

A university administrator speaks in puzzled tones about the "symptoms of mysterious origin" that caused him to be hospitalized for "exhaustive tests that showed nothing. I didn't understand, the doctor didn't understand. . . ." His voice trails off.

Those are the symptoms of frustration.

RESPONSES TO FRUSTRATION

The importance of frustration for Burn-out lies in what one does with it. The way one reacts to frustration has a lot to do with whether or not one will fall deeper into Burn-out and, ultimately, whether or not one can stay in the field. Basically, one can respond to frustration in three ways. One can use it as a source of destructive or constructive energy, or one can just walk away from it, licking one's wounds.

Negative Energy

Margaret B., the schoolteacher whose emotional collapse led to her leaving the field, describes her initial reactions to frustration:

> When I started teaching I worked 12 hours a day. Even in the
> first year or two I saw that it wasn't working out. But I didn't
> slack off. On the contrary, in a desperate effort to turn things
> around, I *increased* my time commitment. All my efforts were
> bent toward warding off impending destruction. I was passion-
> ately committed to maintaining quality at all costs, and for as
> long as I could keep it up I was successful. Maybe I could only
> plan three class trips a year instead of six, but I still gave the
> students the experiences I thought they should have.

"For as long as I could keep it up I was successful." In an effort
to combat frustration this wholly admirable person made herself function at too high an energy level; she eventually brought
herself to a standstill. In the dogged, jut-jawed "last stand"
against frustration that she depicts here lay the origins of the
symptoms that left her professionally disabled.

There is no doubt that frustration creates energy. But
when it is an energy of willful denial, a frenzy of activity aimed
at evading the reality of frustration or doing away with causes
of frustration that are among the "givens" of the situation, then
it is a self-destructive, negative kind of energy. It is one of the
fastest routes to Burn-out. In Margaret's case it led to her giving
up teaching. This outcome is not uncommon. The emotional
exhaustion left in the wake of such desperate energy brings
about many a precipitous departure from the field; the person
often does not even pass through the stage of apathy. The social
worker in Chapter 4 who works 60 to 70 hours a week in an
isolated rural facility to keep from having to think about her life
(as a single woman of 35) is another example of negative energy.
Her prospects for a lasting career in the helping professions are
not good.

Positive Energy

The energy generated by frustration can take a person in
another, more constructive direction. A head nurse in a nursing
home, feeling herself bogged down, looks for a more interesting
job. Unable to obtain one, she begins to work for her B.S.

degree. A paraprofessional drug counselor, tired of being treated as an ex-addict and aware of the limits of his knowledge, scans the case reports filed by psychiatrists and social workers in order to learn a new therapeutic language. Bolstering this self-teaching with outside reading and study, he gains access to staff meetings and wins the grudging respect of the professionals. Promoted to supervisor of counselors, he lobbies for an expansion of the counselors' responsibilities. In retrospect he concludes, "It had gotten to the point where I had to take some risks." A trainee in family counseling tells a similar story:

> At times when I've felt isolated, unappreciated, barely tolerated by the supervisors and staff, I've gone through a cycle of emotions. First I feel that I'm not valuable, and that makes me depressed. When I'm depressed I'm temporarily out of commission; I can't really work. But then the depression turns to anger, and I'm ready to start breaking down doors again. And believe me, I'm not afraid to break down doors. At those moments I realize that change has to come from within myself, from my own strength.

The specific steps these individuals have taken to break out of their frustration, and the sources of strength they have drawn upon, will be discussed more fully in the chapters on Intervention. The important point here is that, by channeling the energy of frustration in a constructive direction, they have made this potentially negative energy work for them. By taking responsibility, confronting issues, and taking actions that may bring about change, they have released some of the emotional tension created by frustration. The cycle of frustration outlined by the family counseling intern—first depression, then anger, then action—is highly instructive. It shows how a person can use frustration— itself a stage of Burn-out—as a springboard out of the Burn-out cycle and back onto a positive career path. Frustration, then, can be a major turning point in the progression through the stages. A person who misses this turn is likely to descend into apathy, from which it is harder to climb out.

The release of energy can serve a positive function even

when the result is less dramatic. A psychologist, who frequently observes public health laws being violated and APA standards not being met at psychiatric hospitals where he is employed part-time, discharges his anger by "sitting down and writing a report or else calling a meeting about it." Sometimes there is some notice taken of his complaint; sometimes there is not. Either way, he has satisfied himself by making a gesture, and that lets him hang in there for the next round.

Withdrawal

Probably the most common response to frustration is not to express it at all, but simply to bottle it up and turn away from the threatening situation. The drug counselor who raised himself to a quasi-professional role did not respond so heroically at the first hint of frustration. At first he "avoided my clients as much as possible, so that they wouldn't learn how little I knew." "Avoided clients"—the phrase comes up again and again. One avoids clients because one has come to dislike or resent them, because one despairs of being able to do anything for them, because one is physically exhausted, because one doesn't want to be "found out" as an ignorant charlatan, or for whatever other reason. Some people catch themselves walking away from their jobs—and from their idealism and concern. Then they get angry, assert themselves, and get back into the center of things. Others—by far the greater number, unfortunately—drift into the fourth and final stage of Burn-out: *Apathy.*

Different people express their frustration in different ways. One "spends half my time, on and off the job, talking about how frustrating it is to be a nurse." Another speaks hesitantly, repeatedly characterizing himself as "uncomfortable" in the position of a human services administrator, but finally leaving unstated that which is more troubling than he cares to say. Both, subject to some opportune intervention, are on the way to apathy.

Chapter 9

THE RETREAT INTO APATHY

"If you could look into a crystal ball and see yourself in ten years working at the same job in the same place as you are now, what would be your gut reaction?" When people working in the helping professions (ranging from paraprofessional addiction counselors to psychiatrists) are asked this question, they give answers like these:

"Just awful."
"I'd feel like an idiot."
"I'd probably be drunk."
"The pits!"
"I couldn't even imagine it."
"Oh, brother!"
"I'd kill myself first."
"Yuk!"
"I'd be dead."
"I'd feel like a caged animal."
"No way!"
"Forget it!"
"Sorry, but it just doesn't fit into my plans."

If the same people were asked how they felt about their work at the present time, it is doubtful that many would be so vehement or so negative. A psychiatric technician just out of college who wanted to become a clinical psychologist might well label his present job "yuk" or "the pits." But what does it mean when a woman of 30 who *is* a clinical psychologist with a doctorate, and who has described herself as generally well satisfied with her work, says this in response to the hypothetical "crystal ball"?

> My reaction in some ways is negative. I couldn't tolerate the exhaustion, boredom, and frustration of the last four years for another ten.

What does it mean when a man of 40 who sits at the top of an administrative pyramid (and thus has no upward promotional path stretching out ahead of him) says this about the prospect of keeping his prestigious job for 10 years?

> I imagine I'd be getting a bit desperate. No, I'm not interested, thank you, unless my present aggravations can be alleviated.

It appears that for some people the 10-year projection into the future serves as a moment of truth about the present. It creates the detachment, the psychological distance, that enables people to "think the unthinkable" and face the dark side of their lives. It is easier to say, "I'd be stagnated doing this 10 years from now" than "I'm stagnated now." A person who rationalizes that a particular job is "great" and who in 10 years probably will rationalize that the same job is "good enough" may yet feel—and be willing to say—that that job would not be such a great one to have in 10 years.

Meanwhile, the person *does* have to cope with that job now and *may* well have to cope with it 10 years from now. When the "crystal ball" question is expanded to include "considered" as well as "gut" reactions, this sometimes unpleasant reality comes into focus. After exclaiming that being at the same job in 10 years would be "unthinkable" or "a fate worse than death," people start to think about whether it really could happen that way. Some insist that it could not possibly happen; they may be right, especially when they are just beginning their careers or when (as with, say, a psychiatrist) they are in a position to exploit many opportunities. Others think again. "Well, it could easily happen," some admit. A young psychiatric technician reflects, "It's possible, though very unlikely—but then again, I've already been at this place longer than the nine months I intended to stay." Some people set conditions (what is called "bargaining with the devil"), e.g., "I guess I can live with it if my responsibilities are expanded," or "if only I can get rid of the administrative garbage and just have the fun part." Some cope by means of humor: "Okay, as long as I'm not treating the very same alcoholics."

Many of these individuals will indeed stay at the same job or the same type of job, accommodating themselves gradually as their aspirations are scaled down by advancing age. To reconcile their aspirations with reality they will look for small signs of progress—promotions, seniority, tenure, periodic pay increases. A schoolteacher in her late 20s is more realistic than most when she concedes, "I could never leave the school system. I need the structure of the job, the order it gives my life." What "structure" means for most people is financial security. A person who has begun raising a family and making payments on a home is not about to walk away from a weekly pay check without having something better in the offing. And if there is nothing better? The top manager who envisioned himself "getting desperate" in his job confessed at the same time to being "financially trapped." This man may be less free to act out his discontents than a counselor I.

When the chief justice of a state supreme court was forced to resign because of alleged improprieties, reporters asked him how he would feel when arguing cases as a private attorney before the court which he once headed. He replied, "It will be distasteful to appear before my former colleagues in court. It is also distasteful not to eat." His bitter words lay bare the dynamic of the stage of *apathy:* a growing disillusionment with the job, together with a growing dependency on the job for survival.

FROM EMPATHY TO APATHY

Apathy takes the form of a progressive emotional detachment in the face of frustration. The starting point, of course, is the enthusiasm, the idealism, the overidentification of the beginner. If one is to come down from the clouds and work effectively, some detachment is desirable—and inevitable. But most workers in the field do not have ideal learning conditions and sympathetic expert guidance to help them reach an optimum level of detachment. Frustration comes as it will, sometimes brutally, and the detachment that develops in its wake is less a poised emotional distancing than a kind of numbness. In "turning off" to frustrating experiences, one may well turn off to people's needs and to one's own caring.

Apathy can be felt as boredom. A private duty nurse working with chronically and terminally ill patients, losing hope of ever seeing a patient improve, finds her mind wandering. A psychologist in private practice laments that "the work gets to be repetitive and boring, especially with a patient who is boring. Sometimes I find myself looking at my watch. Sometimes I get angry and threaten to throw the person out." This from someone who is at the pinnacle of her profession. "I used to feel rejected when people didn't show up for their hour with me," she adds. "Now I'm relieved." Nor does it take many years on the job before a school teacher starts getting up in the morning and looking out the window, hoping for a "snow day."

In an often repeated story, the once-idealistic helper traces the erosion of the desire to help and the feeling of involvement with clients that he or she used to have. For the counselor in an alcohol detox unit, the process may take six months to a year:

> When I started out, I dealt with people mainly at an emotional level and it took its toll. The most frustrating part was working with recidivists. When the same person comes in 30 or 40 times in six months, tying up resources and man hours in futile effort, empathy turns to apathy. I would try to give the same quality of service that I had at the beginning, but I didn't feel the same. I was going through the motions; the emotions weren't there anymore. I used to consider it an honor when clients followed me around and bothered me. Now I just want to duck out and have some time to myself.

For a psychiatric nurse, it may take two or three years:

> I find myself wearing thin, losing tolerance, losing patience. When I first took the job, I would occasionally spend an off-duty day on the unit if I didn't have anything in particular to do. If a patient or a group of patients wanted to talk about a problem in the evening, I might sit and spend a couple of hours with them. I don't do that now. The other night a patient called me at 11:30. Once I would have been glad to talk to her. Now my first reaction was, "For God's sake, what does she want now?" I guess you could say I've started putting myself first.

People who started out caring about others, end up caring mainly about their own health, sanity, peace of mind, and survival.

The shift of focus is accompanied by an attitude of resignation. "I do my job as well as I can," says a counselor in one of the military services, "but whether I'm helping people is questionable." It is not a happy self-assessment. An aide on a psychiatric ward strikes some of the dominant chords of apathy as he relates his growing sense of futility:

> At the beginning, like everybody else, I was gung-ho. I'd wake up thinking, "Here's another day. What can I get done today?" I spent a lot of time with the patients, gathered as much informa-

tion as I could, and tried to work as a team with the rest of the staff. After five or six months, as I found the results I had expected not happening, I got to be indifferent. I'd wake up in the morning and not care about going to work. It was just another day, just a job. I spent less time with patients and did only what was necessary to get by. It was unpleasant having to do things that way, and I got away from it by spending time socializing with the staff instead of working with patients.

"Indifferent," "just another day," "just a job," "did what was necessary to get by," "going through the motions," "putting in time"—with these words empathy has turned to apathy. Expectations have been lowered. The retreat from commitment is on.

That such detachment comes about as a defense against frustration comes through clearly in this account by a college-educated alcoholism counselor in her mid-20s who at one time would "break down and cry" when a client failed to respond:

> I used to go home and worry about my clients at night. I'd talk about cases with my family. I'd lie in bed making plans: "How can I help this person?" "Where can I make a referral?" Now I just turn off; I get disgusted with their behavior and their attitude. If someone misses an appointment, I just think, "Well, that's okay; you'll be back. If you don't come in I'll eventually refer you back to the court. It doesn't make any difference to me whether you come back or not."

This disillusioned worker "shuts off" in the same way to the frustrations of dealing with the top-heavy bureaucracy in her agency. Facing the usual array of unresponsive, obtuse-seeming administrators who "write grants, send memos, and collect their paychecks while letting the staff go out and do the work as best they can," she has had these reactions:

> At first I'd get angry at the way they were putting clients last on their priority list. I'd get angry and talk to my supervisor about it. Then I saw that nothing ever happened as a result. Now it doesn't make any difference anymore.

This is the cycle of emotions that leads down the road to apathy. First anger, then attempted remedial action, then recognition of failure and futility, and finally indifference. At the end of Chapter 8 we saw how frustration could touch off a cycle of emotions culminating in the release of positive energy, that is, from depression to anger to constructive action. Perhaps the difference is that the family counseling trainee in Chapter 8 whose anger led to her "breaking down doors" has not yet experienced the last stage of the cycle—namely, the realization that her actions will not make much difference in the long run. What is more likely is that, being older, more experienced, and more strong-willed (even though new to the field) than the apathetic alcoholism counselor, she has taken more effective action than simply complaining to her supervisor. In any case, the difference between the two accounts is instructive. What does one do in response to frustration? Some attack, while others retreat.

APATHY IN THE RAW: THE "DRUG-FREE" COUNSELOR

At several points in our discussion the recently "drug-free" addict who is hired to "relate to" his or her fellow sufferers as a rehabilitation counselor has proved a useful barometer of Burn-out among helping professionals generally. Nowhere is this more true than in the stage of apathy. The speed with which disillusionment overtakes the untrained, overworked paraprofessional, the lack of career alternatives or an educational investment to protect, and the availability of an easy way out (i.e., resuming drug use) make the addict turned counselor a prime candidate for quick and dramatic Burn-Out.

Roger F., whose career we have followed through the three prior stages of Burn-out, has had a taste of apathy as well:

> While I was experiencing the frustration of seeing my own ineffectiveness repeatedly demonstrated, what were my fellow ex-

addict counselors doing? It didn't take me long to find out. One evening in the shower room I saw a group of them drink a bottle of gin before doing a group. Then, after loading up on chewing gum, cigarettes, and mouthwash, they went in to work with their clients. Afterward they laughed and said things like, "Boy, I'm glad I was a little high; otherwise I don't know if I could have handled that meeting."

I never drank on the job like that. I never abused alcohol or went back to using drugs, as some of the other counselors did. But I quickly was corrupted by the attitude behind that behavior. "Good," I told myself, "I guess I don't have to be perfect." I could come to work late, take long lunches, fall behind on my paper work and whatever else I considered unpleasant. That I did those things was my responsibility, but it was easy not to take responsibility in an environment where no one else took responsibility. I felt I did not have to live up to my original high standards because I did not see others maintaining those standards. I was co-opted by the group norms.

As a result, I got into some pretty serious deviance myself. Addicts would come in offering the counselors coats, tires, stereos at bargain prices—no questions asked. I bought a few of those. It was also common practice for male counselors to take advantage of women addicts sexually. I did that, too. Eventually I got caught and was suspended for six weeks.

I was responsible for the things I did, but I don't blame myself or the other counselors. What we did was only natural under the circumstances. For all the good we were able to do as counselors, we might as well not have been there. Sure, it was better than being in jail, but so is any job.

Apathy. A job is a job is a job.

One of Roger's colleagues who did engage in the on-the-job drinking Roger describes is Fred R., who came to the state-run treatment center from Daytop Village in 1970 with "all the answers" but with no formal training. After experiencing the kinds of frustrations with which we are by now familiar, he became cynical about his work and the people he worked with. "Methadone didn't change people's lives," he observed. "Most of the addicts came in high on alcohol. They weren't interested in the groups or the counseling; they just wanted their medication. All we were doing was maintaining them." Amid the intoxication that was prevalent among both the addicts and the counselors, Fred began spending his off-hours in bars and taking swigs with his fellow counselors in the shower room. Alcohol became what heroin had once been for him. For a short time his job had taken the place of the drug, but the glow soon faded:

> I became pessimistic about whether anybody could get well. At first, if someone didn't make it, I felt as if I had lost a friend. After a while I just shrugged my shoulders. I stopped caring about running groups or doing anything at the center. Instead, I just collected my pay check and looked forward to the end of the day. Half the time I didn't want to be there at all.

His drinking increasingly caused problems for him on the job, and after a blowup with his supervisor he was fired. "Bottoming out" as an alcoholic, he later came back into the field in the equally precarious role of an alcoholism counselor. Since then he has been going to school to obtain professional credentials. He also has had one alcoholic relapse which necessitated his taking a "retreat" of several weeks and returning to a job at a different facility.

Fred's story, with its "stumbles" and "falls" and its up-and-down recovery track, is a common one in his field. As rehabilitation program administrators throughout the country have begun to realize, the status of a drug or alcohol counselor is an inherently unstable one. It cannot be called a career because it does not offer the satisfactions that almost everyone sooner or later wants from life. As a result, recovering substance abusers who serve as counselors without formal training find within two or three years that they must go forward (by gaining knowledge that enables them to improve themselves professionally) or backward (to the deviant behavior that they know so well). As one who moved forward to become a counseling administrator put it,

> You can't get away with the jive stuff that you could throw at people in 1967 or 1970. Clients are more sophisticated now. They reject counselors who try to get by on the old street language. Counselors who don't keep learning new skills end up hurting themselves as well as their clients.

He estimates that for every counselor who learns new skills and progresses into a career, three others revert to drug use. It is the rare counselor who stays on the job as a paraprofessional even for five years.

The first decade of drug rehabilitation programs, beginning in the late 1960s, was a stormy one. The following account of a large city-run program in those early years (given by a counselor who worked there) may sound like a case of nostalgic embellishment, but there have been too many such reminiscences concerning too many programs for us to be able to doubt its accuracy:

> The clinic in those days was *wild.* Counselors were out on the sidewalk pitching dimes with clients for money. What with the counselors getting high on reefers during lunch break, everybody was walking around spaced out, staff and clients alike. Some of the counselors were "the world owes me a living" types who operated just as they had on the street. One counselor was caught selling urine specimens. Another one, who was always boozing, used to harrass women addicts from the moment they walked in the door. One day he picked up a chair and knocked it over a desk. He was given a warning. The next day he again came in drunk and was fired.
>
> It was scandalous. The only thing that was required in those days was to have the records straight when NIDA or the FDA came around. Nobody even used the word "treatment," and nobody understood what the word "rehabilitation" meant. It was just an assembly line where people came in for their methadone so they could sell it out on the street.
>
> There were guns and knives all over the place. Just when the hospital staff was about to go on strike to have the drug clinic moved out of the hospital and put on an island somewhere, a client was shot right in the clinic. After that they put in a metal detector. Not many people would walk in there looking for a job, and nobody would stay just for the pay check—unless they had to.

It is a portrait of a leaderless, permissive, *laissez faire* organization, one where no one took responsibility. It is a portrait of mass apathy.

Since that time the people who run drug programs have learned from their mistakes (as well as from growing public awareness of the "scandalous" character of their earlier undertakings). Numerous organizational interventions have brought the chaotic atmosphere described here under some degree of control. These reforms include hiring better-trained people as counselors and paying them more, ending the take-home distribution of methadone, requiring that addicts pay for methadone (thus giving them an incentive to detoxify), and requiring that addicts be on time—to the minute—to receive their methadone as they once had to be on time for their "dope drops." Procedures are more orderly, and clients and counselors alike are treated with greater respect. Clinic practices vary according to the region and the source of funding, but in most places the heyday of the drunken, violent counselor in the crime-ridden clinic is over.

This simply means, of course, that drug rehab counselors now only have the same problems as nurses, teachers, psychologists, and others working in "civilized" institutions—problems such as case overload, political power plays, bureaucratic insensitivity, paper work, administrative tie-ups, and the competitive struggle for career advancement. Welcome to the real world!

GROUP APATHY: THE PSYCHIATRIC WARD

Earlier in this chapter we heard from a discouraged psychiatric aide, Marvin D., who "got away from it by spending time socializing with the staff instead of working with patients." The rest of the staff, meanwhile, got away from "it" by socializing with *him*. People who share the same experiences and have similar frustrations naturally are receptive to each other's complaints. Like those spirited accounts of bullets whizzing and liquor flowing at the drug clinic, Marvin's description of team meetings on the ward is a portrait of group apathy:

> We have some hopelessly psychotic patients whom nobody can
> help. At our team meetings there is really very little discussion
> of these patients. Everybody just sits around with their heads
> down, waiting for somebody else to respond to the questions,
> somebody else to take the initiative. What can you do? There is
> no spontaneity, no energy. You can feel the apathy in the air.

If the phrase "Where's it going to get you?" symbolizes stagnation, the essence of apathy is captured by the deadly words
"What can you do?" The two sentiments are equally contagious.

Apathy (like enthusiasm, stagnation, and frustration) is a
collective as well as individual experience, and different groups
of workers have their own ways of expressing it—and of trying
to break out of it. Marvin goes on to recount the sporadic
attempts made by the staff on his ward to lift themselves out
of their apathy:

> We go along for a while, and then all the complaining about the
> doctors and the hospital starts getting channeled into personal
> quarrels. We pick fights with one another. When the tension rises
> to an uncomfortable level a meeting is called. At the meeting we
> all air our feelings, our opinions, our perceptions. We end by
> making a commitment to be more open with one another. It
> works for a while, and then we settle back into our old roles,
> where we just don't expend ourselves, don't put ourselves out to
> communicate. Nothing is resolved.

Here we see a group going through the same cycle of futility
that we observed when an individual periodically rises up to
question "the system," only to sink back into lethargy when
nothing happens. After a while the person or group does not
bother to get aroused anymore. Marvin's staff meetings are like
an informal version of the "workshop highs" discussed in the
following chapter, where workers are given some time off to air
their frustrations, release tension, and meet some new people.
As Marvin says, "It works for a while," but it does not take long
for the high to wear off when people return to the same old job
in the same old place. And that only makes things worse.

In our analysis of the spread of stagnation we briefly looked in on an inpatient psychiatric ward that serves as a training ground for resident physicians in that specialty. The unusual feature of this situation, where the physicians are both inexperienced and transient, is the amount of responsibility for patient care that the nursing staff must take on—responsibility that is a source of both pride and vexation for the staff. This is one helping facility where there is some real *esprit de corps.* Experienced nurses and aides teach newcomers to do a good job, to put out some effort, to try to avoid being discouraged. Those who care about the patients and want to help them are supported by their peers as they seek to learn how they can be most effective. In other words, the group has come together around positive rather than negative values—caring rather than indifference, energy rather than defeatism.

Does this mean that there is no Burn-out here, that nobody ever gets to the stage of apathy? Hardly. For there is still case overload; there are still insensitive supervisors and administrators; there are still the frustration and the tragedy of dealing with fellow human beings who have lost contact with what we accept as reality. Most of all, there are the doctors—psychiatric residents doing their one-year stint on their way to bigger and better things. Privileged, confident, emotionally uninvolved, they are an irritant to the hard-pressed nurses and aides. In the eyes of the staff the residents are callous prima donnas who do not spend enough time on the ward to know what is going on. A disgruntled staff member complains, "The system here is set up to give the residents 'experience.' It's their bowl of cherries. The patients are guinea pigs, and the staff are pack animals. Why do I stay here? To protect the patients from those narcissistic bastards."

For this group, the cost of their close-knit spirit and constructive cooperation with one another is a shared sense of grievance that locks them into the disillusionment cycle. Instead of supporting one another in accepting the "givens" of the situation and taking responsibility for what they can accomplish, they support one another in blaming the doctors for what cannot be accomplished. Setting impossibly high standards for themselves, they bewail the futility of their efforts instead of looking for the small differences that their actions can make. Although not alienated from one another, they are alienated together—alienated *with* and *by* one another. For them it's "us against the world." And this negativism undercuts the positive spirit of their relations with one another and with patients.

Another factor contributing to Burn-out on this ward is the annual turnover of the psychiatric residents. The residents move on after a year, leaving the nurses and technicians to pick up the pieces. Each July, when one group of residents leaves and another comes in, whatever mutual accommodations and working relationships the staff has built up with the previous residents must be rebuilt from scratch. As one of the nurses rather grandiloquently put it, "No sooner do we get them trained than they're gone." This lack of continuity leads to what a technician called "built-in frustration and disappointment." It also leads to a high annual turnover rate among the staff. In the initial period of confusion and discouragement that follows the changeover of residents in July, about one-quarter to one-third of the staff decide that it is time to go elsewhere. This further demoralizes the remaining staff members, who in a stressful period would want to be able to continue working with people they are comfortable with. At this rate the staff turns over almost completely every three years. In the words of a technician who left to work on a crisis line,

> The good year was my first year. That's when I formed the bonds with my peers. The second year it was like a new class coming in. If I'd stayed a third year, there would have been fewer people yet with whom I would have shared those important learning experiences that bring people together.

It is well known that Burn-out is a prime cause of turnover. What we have here is a vicious cycle where turnover is both a *cause* and a *result* of Burn-out. Resident turnover leads to staff Burn-out, which leads to staff turnover, which leads to more staff Burn-out, which leads to more turnover, and so on. This is not to mention the effects of such upheaval on the patients.

In the end, young, highly motivated, concerned people find themselves going through the four stages of disillusionment in anywhere from six months to two or three years—about as long as it takes an untrained addiction counselor. These are not "old-timers." They are people in their 20s who have discovered what apathy is:

> "There would be days when I'd go to work only because I didn't want to let the rest of the staff down. Why should I put in a nine- or ten-hour day and get nothing back?"
> "I have to ask myself why I'm doing this. It's the people I work with and the people I'm there to help. Sometimes that's not enough."

CO-OPTATION: THE OLD-TIMER AND THE NOVICE

In telling how his own behavior was influenced by observing other drug counselors act out their apathy, Roger F. described himself as being "co-opted by the group norms." We have already seen the co-optation process in the stage of stagnation, where the message was, "Slow down. Stop running so fast. You can't accomplish much anyway." In the stage of apathy a deeper message of hopelessness and despair is conveyed.

This is not to say that we can precisely distinguish between the contagions that occur in the two stages. It is not as if the enthusiastic novice picks up stagnation by talking to one group of people and then apathy by talking to another. Usually it is from people who are quite far gone into apathy that one learns the attitudes associated with stagnation. One does not immediately become apathetic oneself because from enthusiasm to apathy is too far to go in one leap. One has to pass through stagnation and frustration first. Thus, when we talk about the co-optation of inexperienced personnel by veteran staff members, we are seeing two sides of the same picture. From the newcomer's side, what we see is stagnation. From the old-timer's point of view, we are looking through the lenses of apathy.

Who are the people doing the co-opting? Usually they are people who long ago made a decision—sometimes consciously, sometimes not—to give up and drift with the tide. They are, for instance, the psychiatric nurses and aides about whom the psychiatrist quoted in Chapter 6 remarked, "Some of these people are 'institutionalized'; when they've been there for 30 years it gets hard to tell them apart from the patients." Such comments, directed at senior nurses, teachers, prison guards, or social workers, can become self-fulfilling prophecies. They accurately describe some of these people, while at the same time they create a mold for them to fit into. Perhaps this stereotyping is one of the only ways younger staff members can fight back against the near-irresistible force of mass apathy.

The newcomer in the full flush of enthusiasm hardly gives a passing glance to the apathetic old-timer. The person who is still young and fresh, but who has had a sobering taste of disillusionment, looks upon the defeated elder with an outward contempt and a deep-seated fear. A counselor at a state correctional facility says, "I see the ten-year men mechanically going through their duties. If it could happen to them, it might happen to me. I have to ask myself what I'm going to do to prevent it." Marvin, the psychiatric aide, catches himself in the middle of his saga of disillusionment and takes a moment to disassociate himself from the old-timers:

> After a while you get to thinking, "It's just a job; it's just another day." Eventually you're just going through the motions. I mean, it's not *that* bad. I haven't gotten to that point yet, but eventually you do.

What he means to say is that he feels stagnated but not apathetic. Apathy is not an easy thing to admit to. "You" can be apathetic, but "I" am not—yet. Marvin's "you" refers to the older staff members that he observes, and also to what he himself might in time become. In the lethargic, ill-tempered complainer at the next desk one sees a reflected image of oneself in the all too possible future.

There is a children's game that goes: "Scissors cuts paper. Rock breaks scissors. Paper covers rock." To this could be added, "Apathy drains enthusiasm." When two people, one of them with a virulent respiratory infection, are put in a small, badly ventilated room, the well person "catches" the sick person's illness; the sick person does not "catch" the well person's health. So it is with the contagion of Burn-out. The contest for influence between the old-timer and the novice is no contest. In the acculturation that goes on wherever people work together, the worldly old hand who "cuts corners" and "gets by" is the native, while the bright-eyed enthusiast is the bewildered immigrant. Day in and day out, singling out the overly conscientious with names like "Supercounselor" or "Airman of the Month," established staff members let newcomers know "the way things are" and hold the threat of alienation over those who would aspire beyond the limits set by "the system."

Apathetic senior staff members gain the upper hand over inexperienced colleagues for a number of reasons. There are usually more of them. They have been there longer, and thus can speak sometimes with the authority of position and always with the authority of experience. They have been apathetic a long time, while the enthusiast has become that way overnight. Unlike enthusiasm, which tends to be as shallow as it is intense, apathy is a stable attitude, one that imbeds itself deeply in a person's character. Last but not least, the reality of the situation favors the apathetic point of view, and only in part because attitudes of disillusionment and despair are self-fulfilling. It *is* tough to get the job done in the human services.

The Choice: Adapt or Perish

The prison counselor who looked askance at the "ten-year men" in his facility takes this view of the co-optation process:

> It's good for the organization to have enthusiastic new people coming in, but I hope for their sake that it doesn't take them as long to see the reality as it took me. Either you learn to adapt, learn the bureaucratic ropes, or you leave—as many do, judging from our high turnover rate. Those who stay find their niche and become part of the system. I wonder to what extent that's true of me. I know that if I continued to buck the system as I did at first, I'd be in the nuthouse.

This man, in his highly conscious, self-questioning way, is attempting to find a middle ground—that of negotiating the realization of some of his ideals within the constraints of the system. It is a difficult course to steer.

A top-level administrator in a state-run human services program who has a good vantage point for observing many levels of bureaucracy sees these same three choices facing would-be managers. He lists three types of people in his organization:

> There are some who accept the system completely. These are born bureaucrats who are cautious from the start. Lacking ambition and uninterested in achieving particular goals, they look for a comfortable position to retire into, a place where nobody cares too much about what they're doing. Then there are those who take on the system, such as a friend of mine who is now in the hospital. Finally, there are a few, the ones with a better political sense, who seem to be able to accomplish something without upsetting everyone around them. These are the ones who can find routes of compromise.

A former teacher says, "There were others besides myself who sought to stimulate the students. All of them have since left or become part of the mainstream." Reports like hers come in from every sector of the help-giving fields. At some point everyone has to make a value judgment about whether to accept the "givens" and put up with the hassles or leave the field.

Once within the mainstream, one has another value judgment to make. A social work supervisor in an alcohol detox unit says of her staff, "Some are here to help; some are here for the cash. Some cope by being committed to doing the best they can; some cope by complaining." Even with all the frustrations, some people find maneuvering room within the mainstream to achieve limited goals. For them, the "givens" are the first but not the last word—the rules of the game, not the final score. The alternative is to retreat into apathy. One can accept the "givens" so completely that one simply gives up.

GIVING UP: RETREAT AND SURVIVAL

Giving Up the Job

Apathy is no fun. When one's work is no longer meaningful, one naturally feels the impulse to walk out. A nurse who acted on that impulse tells what it feels like to have reached the end of the line:

> I went into nursing because I didn't like to see people sick. Well, as a nurse that's all I ever saw. I was always working with people who were dying or in pain. I reacted either by getting very emotional, which meant that I would be a wreck by the time I went home each day (sometimes I would be physically ill), or by shutting off completely.
>
> On my last job I was working in a suite of four rooms on a male medical floor. In one room was a middle-aged man who was dying from cirrhosis of the liver. Next door was someone with cancer who was on the way out. Across the hall was a recent stroke victim who, like the others, was really not that old. Next door to him was a man in his late 50s who a month before had been functioning as you and I are. Since he had been admitted to the hospital with a mysterious combination of symptoms, everything possible had gone wrong with him, and he was now comatose. Every day I would go in and tend to those patients. Every day I would walk down the halls past other rooms and listen to the moans. One night I finally had had it. I sat down on the floor in the middle of that suite, outside those four doors, and buried my head in my hands for 15 minutes. I walked out of the hospital that night and have never gone back.

A resident at that hospital walked out, too—in his case not because of the pain of being exposed to incurable illness, but because of institutional and peer disapproval of his unorthodox handling of cases, which involved less diagnostic testing and more old-fashioned bedside contact than "the system" allowed for:

> It got to the point where they were waiting for me to make a mistake. When it appeared that I had made one, a memo critical of my actions was circulated. The administration waited before supporting me until it had been proved that I had not in fact made a mistake. Sooner or later, though, I would make one. Why wait around to be hung? I was getting tired of it, too. The energy required of me to act according to my principles within that structure was too much. I was coming home drained. Sure, I'll accept certain sacrifices in order to do some good for people. But who wants to be a martyr? I sure as hell don't.

Words like "getting tired of it," "drained," and "martyr" convey this physician's response to a particular frustration, which was to pack up his tents and retreat rather than take on the system. In his case, though, there was the option of retreating to something better. Having completed his required residency period, he could take a staff position at another hospital. Would he find less institutional conflict and more autonomy there? In private practice? As a sub-specialist? In the heat of his reaction to a hospital's procedures and to his powerless position there, he may not have considered that he would be facing new hassles, new complications, and new choices with every new opportunity he might take up.

Having other opportunities makes one more likely to leave a particular job in response to encroaching apathy, but less likely to leave the field altogether. A psychiatrist who can divide his or her time among private practice, teaching, writing, hospital consultantships, and running a drug clinic is not about to burn out of that career. A doctor or lawyer has made a larger educational investment and gets more satisfactions from the job (higher pay, status, and power, for starters) than a paraprofessional addiction counselor, who has little to lose by walking out. A nurse, say, would stand somewhere between these two extremes. The higher one rises in the hierarchy, the more carefully one will consider the options before resigning. Age, too, is a factor. Investment of time in a job or career is a strong disincentive to giving it up. After a while, what else can one do? Staying on the job becomes a matter of survival.

Giving Up—on the Job

A government planner in her late 20s remarks, "People dig themselves into a rut. They create their own dead ends by staying in the same place forever. As soon as I stop learning new things on a job, as soon as I have a vested interest in the status quo, I feel it's time to move on." Her criteria are useful ones that can serve as a constructive intervention against apathy. What she does not say (and may or may not realize) is that, once she is past the near-automatic early stages of career advancement, the new jobs she would like to move on to may not be waiting for her.

In military service one probably will get promoted from Airman to Airman First Class or from Second to First Lieutenant simply by putting in one's time, following all the rules, and never going AWOL. One may never get promoted from Technical Sergeant to Master Sergeant or from Major to Lieutenant Colonel, since stringent quotas create stiff competition at those grade levels. Much the same is true in civilian life when it comes to seeking either a promotion or a new job. When this government planner is no longer a hotshot just out of college with untold potential, she may not be as attractive to potential employers as she is now. In addition, she may have taken on family responsibilities that compel her to think in terms of financial security. Thus she may not be in a position to carry out her admirable (and sensible) plan of staying at a job only as long as it remains fresh and challenging. We recall the anguished disclaimers of people who were asked what it would be like to be at the same job in 10 years, together with the words of the ex-judge facing the humiliation of pleading cases before his former colleagues on the bench: "It is also distasteful not to eat."

What then? The most severe, and saddest, form of apathy is that which one experiences when one remains at a job for one reason only: because one needs the job to survive. One has seen what is going on, but one has no inclination to try to change it. Certainly one will not "rock the boat" or take any risks when one can just go along, protecting one's position while doing as little as possible. Security has become the prime concern. "Be careful, you have a state government job," cautions the inner voice. One has given up.

Of all the stages of Burn-out, apathy is the hardest to bounce back from, the one against which it is most difficult to intervene successfully. It is the most settled, the most deep-seated, the one that takes the longest to arrive at and that lasts the longest. It stems from a decision, reached over a period of time and reinforced by one's peers, to stop caring. In the absence of a major personal upheaval, vastly changed conditions on the job, or a concerted intervention, it can last forever.

Moral Detachment

An important factor in this long-range accommodation to a difficult reality is the blunting of the moral concern with which one originally entered the helping fields. This occurs at all levels, from paraprofessional to professional. It has been commonly observed, for example (and confirmed by attitude surveys), that medical students tend to be transformed by their education and training. Generally speaking, they enter medical school as humanists and come out as "scientists" in a very limited sense (in some cases, perhaps, technicians). Four years of professional training (let alone later experience) narrow the focus of their concern from the large moral issue of relieving suffering to measurable, quantifiable, "value-neutral" questions.

Lawyers go through a similar evolution in the course of their careers. What makes the young idealist down the block give up working for Legal Aid after three or four years to join a conventional law practice? Why do some of the noted "radical" lawyers who defend unpopular causes and disadvantaged clients come across to the public as "sharp operators"? A lawyer who has been on many sides of the legal-judicial fence suggests some answers:

> Lawyers are exposed to a number of disillusioning experiences. They get an inside look at the seamy side of life—what people will do to each other for a buck. In our adversary system they learn that any argument they make can be turned on its head. Indeed, they themselves have to anticipate the opposing arguments in order to rebut them. Through such daily practice lawyers learn the relativity of virtue.
>
> Jockeying in such a world, you become a manipulator, whatever else you may be. You may keep your ideals as well, and then again you may not. When you work for Legal Aid, you see how little can be done to realize any ideals. Most of the time you're not even acting as a lawyer; you're just making phone calls to fix things up for people. Once your clients are out of the jam they drop out of sight, and you don't really see whether or how much you've helped them. Amid all this tinkering you hope you'll hit a big case that will change a point of law, but it's the rare lawyer who is so fortunate. So why not quit Legal Aid and go to work for a firm? You don't burn out very easily in a profession where you make $15,000 to start and perhaps $80,000 by the end.

This attorney's concern about the effects of exposure to "the seamy side of life"—an occupational hazard throughout the helping professions—is echoed, with a different slant, by a physician in family practice:

As family doctors we learn about people's lives in detail, including things we can't change, things that are irreducibly bad. Putting ourselves on the line to find out "too much" about people is an emotional risk. We have to make a basic choice. Do we want to say that our job is limited to specific medical-surgical aspects of people's health care? Or do we want to deal with "what's so" for people, to witness things as they really are, in order to account more completely for people's reactions and assist them more effectively. Becoming a family doctor implies making the latter choice, and I feel that my experience has affirmed that choice. My work is enriched by things I learn, even things I don't like. Just because I chose not to see something wouldn't mean that it wasn't there.

A family doctor, like a family lawyer, routinely witnesses marital problems, selfishness and venality within families, destructive family dynamics, alcoholism, and other unsettling realities that he or she would prefer not to see. The human being inside the physician is then vulnerable to being disturbed, to being hurt, and perhaps (in self-protective reaction) to being calloused. The dangers are those of feeling too much or feeling too little. This particular physician has made the value judgment of opening himself to the realities about people and dealing with his own emotional reactions as they occur. Is this any different from the choice that anyone working in the human services has to make? One needs to come to terms with what people are, with the many things people can be—not only as patients or clients, but as colleagues, subordinates, supervisors, administrators, trustees, taxpayers. Not to see the reality is to be primed for disillusionment. To see but not accept the reality is to be frustrated and, finally, apathetic.

THROUGH THE FOUR STAGES: THE CASE OF A BURNED-OUT SOCIAL WORKER

Over the past seven chapters we have gone through the four stages of Burn-out with Roger F., the drug counselor. Another case in which the stage-by-stage process appears with special clarity is that of Lynn M., a social worker with a bachelor's degree in sociology. Lynn, who grew up in poverty, went into the helping professions because she saw "what a difference it had made to my life to have had someone there to help my family."

After graduating from college Lynn went to work for the state welfare department. Her job, which involved helping families meet their financial needs and resolve family conflicts, was "exactly what I wanted to do." She looked forward to being able to "help people improve their lives as much as I could." This was the stage of *enthusiasm*. Lynn, like others in that stage, tended to be overly available and to overidentify with her clients. She cites a case example:

> In one family the father was wasting away with an incurable disease while the mother was a very dependent alcoholic who had begun to abuse her three children after her husband became ill. She herself called and asked for help so that she wouldn't hurt her children. At first this seemed like the ideal opportunity. Here was a family that was asking for services and that was cooperative and responsive. As time went on, though, I realized that I was being drawn into a web. I was seeing this family, especially the woman, several times a week. She would call me in the evenings when she was drunk and ask me to come out and see her. I realized that my being so available was just enabling her to remain what she was. She was transferring her dependency from her husband to me.

Making herself so accessible to this family and others was not helping Lynn, either. When she got home after a long day of listening to other people's problems she did not have enough patience left to listen to her own family. "I don't want to hear about it," she would say. Meanwhile, she could not help noticing that a number of old school friends whom she considered less competent than herself, and who were working in less sensitive areas, were beginning to bring home considerably more money. Each year the gap widened. Lynn felt that her pay was too low for someone who was making important decisions on questions such as child placement. As her expectations shrank to normal proportions and her personal discontents began to surface, Lynn found herself in the stage of *stagnation.*

Handling one inconclusive case after another, Lynn saw that she was not working any miracles. With little training in psychology, she was in over her head when she confronted the complex psychodynamics of families. People seemed to think that she would "walk into a situation that had been building up for 15 years and straighten it out in a day." The federal government, meanwhile, "attached such mind-boggling paper work requirements to everything involving welfare that if I did it all I'd never have time to go out and talk to anyone. So I just did what I absolutely had to." Her difficulties multiplying, she began to experience *frustration.*

No longer was she so concerned about doing the best job she could. She was frankly bored and wanted to find another job. With families she became "less and less tolerant, less and less sympathetic." Looking back, she would trace her progressive detachment from her job in the history of her dealings with one family:

> This woman had a boyfriend who moved in and out. While he was living with her he gave her a lot of support with her children. Whenever they quarreled and he walked out, she'd call me in despair. At first I would go out and spend two hours saying whatever was needed to lift her out of her misery. This happened pretty regularly every few months, and after a year or so I became less responsive to her. Instead of going to see her I'd talk to her on the phone. "So he left again," I'd tell her. "He's left before." If she remained upset I'd tell her I'd be out to see her within a few days. Sometimes I never did go. I was beginning to put things off, and some things weren't getting done at all.

Follow-up visits were an easy thing to put off:

> We had a lot of cases of teenagers who couldn't get along with their parents. The kid would say, "I can't go on living here!" The

parent would say, "You've got to get her out of here! I can't control her anymore!" Usually I would place the child with foster parents, but it would only be temporary. The same problems would recur with the new family, who would be on the phone with the same complaints within a month or two. By that point the original home situation usually had calmed down, and the parents would take the child back.

When I was just starting out, I would keep going back to visit the family and see how they were doing. I would arrange for followup counseling with a private agency and make sure the family actually went there. Later my attitude changed. If the family didn't call me, I didn't call them. It was easier to assume that everything was okay; if it wasn't, I didn't want to know about it. I hoped I'd never hear from them again. Unfortunately, things usually were not okay, and we'd have the family back in our laps some months later. I just hoped they would be assigned to someone else.

Placed in a difficult, discouraging situation, Lynn coped by avoidance and withdrawal. She would cut corners and rationalize that "everything was okay." She had fallen into the stage of *apathy.*

Then a new job opened up in a state agency dealing with child abuse, a problem to which Lynn's work already had given her considerable exposure. Lynn took the job in the hope that it would enable her to focus her energies on one issue. Besides, she did not have anything better to do. She went into the job without clear expectations about what she might accomplish, but the mere change of scene gave her a brief burst of renewed enthusiasm. In fact, she was moving from one set of frustrations to other, more intense ones. In retrospect Lynn concludes,

Protecting children from abuse is an impossible job. When you interview for the job they don't tell you that you won't have the power to carry out the life-and-death decisions you are responsible for making. You don't get sufficient time, resources, or access to information. Not only are the families hostile, but private agencies, knowing how resistant these families are, don't want to deal with them. The police won't get involved unless you have

specific evidence of abuse. And you can't get the evidence because people in the community are a lot more willing to de-
nounce child abuse than to stand up in court and say, "I saw this
happen." I've felt uncomfortable leaving a child in a house where
something questionable has happened: did she fall down the
stairs or was she pushed? But neither the doctors nor the police
would go out on a limb.

"No support for important decisions" was a major frustration in Lynn's case. Her response was to scale down her expectations:

It's frustrating when you realize how much needs to be done, but
can't do anything about it. You start setting limited goals. Instead of expecting a mother and father to straighten out their
relationship with their daughter—or just *talk* to her, even—you
get them to sweep their living room every day.

She had to stay within the narrow limits of her job as a child
abuse investigator, and this, too, was frustrating:

With a teenager the abuse often is an isolated incident, but the
family problems that caused it are not. A 14-year-old girl complained that her father had beaten her black and blue with a belt
because he disapproved of the boys she was dating. The girl was
placed in another home, the father arrested. In time, after her
parents had been visiting her, the girl returned home. Her father
didn't hit her anymore, but that was as far as it went. I couldn't
get him to reexamine his attitude toward her dating behavior, for
instance. They still argued, and a few years later she ran away
and refused to go back. Generally, all I could do was to stop
isolated incidents of physical abuse. Sometimes I couldn't even
do that. The beatings went on; they just weren't reported.

By now Lynn was disillusioned and depressed. "You get
to feeling that there's no point in trying anymore, that there's
very little you can do, that the situation will change or not
change of its own accord whether you're there or not." On the

job she felt "alienated." She stopped trying to reach out to help clients. "Why reach out when you won't get any support from the family, the community, or even your co-workers?" It was easier just to tell people what they wanted to hear and leave the difficult decisions to others. Her cynicism extended to politics and other social causes in which she had previously been active. "Things will go the way they will," she decided. She became, by her own testimony, a complainer, a difficult person to live with.

On top of all this, her career in the agency was at a dead end. "They know damn well," she recalls bitterly,

> ... that people burn out on this job within three years. But it's such a difficult job, and so few people want to do it, that if you can do it at all they won't let you do anything else. They figure it's better to have an apathetic person than no one at all. So if you're good at what you do, even if you've knocked yourself out for years, you're penalized by being stuck. The only alternative is to be made a supervisor, and believe me, that's no promotion. Then you have to talk to *everybody's* clients on the phone instead of just your own. And when all you do is talk on the phone and go out to see if somebody's still alive, it's time to quit.

During a hiring freeze caused by budgetary difficulties that lasted several years, the state kept everyone on the same job indefinitely for want of replacements. Paradoxically, the freeze kept staff morale higher than it might otherwise have been, since it kept intact a congenial, closely knit group of employees. When the freeze ended, the turnover rate shot up, since jobs in other state agencies were now easier to find. The agency saw an influx of new personnel and the nucleus of experienced workers shrank. Lynn looked enviously at those who left to take other positions. She wanted to be part of the turnover. Now, five years out of college, she was almost ready to quit her second job without any assurance that she could get a third.

Twice disillusioned, Lynn was getting near the point where

"a job is a job is a job." Whether she would sink deeper into apathy or find an alternative that would revive her enthusiasm within a framework of more realistic expectations would depend on the next stage of the process: *Intervention.* Moving from the welfare department to child abuse services had been a stopgap intervention, one that had had no lasting effects. There were, however, more constructive interventions available to Lynn—and to others in similar situations.

REALISTIC VS. UNREALISTIC
INTERVENTIONS

What does one do when one finds oneself in one of the four stages of Burn-out? The answer, whatever it is, is a form of *intervention.* Intervention means the steps that are taken— consciously or not, constructively or not—to break the cycle of disillusionment.

Intervention may be self-initiated or may occur in response to an immediate frustration or threat. It may be fueled in part by one's own strength and in part by support and guidance (sometimes *mis*guidance) from peers, supervisors, family and friends, or whoever else is important in one's life. It may be a temporary stopgap or a real change.

Intervention can—and should—occur at any of the four stages of disillusionment. One of the main tasks of trainers and supervisors should be to help staff members experience the four stages with greater awareness and thus be less subject to violent swings of emotion. In reality, though, as we have noted, inter- vention most often takes place (if at all) at the stage of frustra- tion, when it is almost too late. In the stage of enthusiasm people are having too good a time to see any need for intervention. Stagnation does not usually provide the energy required to change course, though interventions in the areas of further education, skill development, and career advancement are sometimes initiated at this stage. As for apathy, that stage is already a long way down into disillusionment, and the road back up is a long, hard one which some people negotiate successfully but many never attempt.

Most often it is frustration that moves a person off center and impels change. Frustration is not so bad when it gets people angry enough to break out of a bad situation instead of becoming apathetic. But our aim in exploring the entire Burn-out process is to help make it possible to intervene before as well as after the stage of frustration is reached.

It is in this sense that the recommendations in this and the following chapter are intended as much for managers and administrators as for the individual worker. Those who have supervisory roles in human services organizations will want to be aware of Burn-out in their staff and to be able (both in a preventive and remedial sense) to show staff members how they can do something about it.

This is not the same as saying that solutions to Burn-out will come primarily through structural changes in organizations (e.g., in work hours, distribution of responsibilities, and patterns of authority and communication). Christina Maslach,[1] for example, finds that Burn-out is less severe in facilities with lower client-to-staff ratios. But how can administrators act on this finding at a time when their budgets are being cut? Although recognizing that there is no all-encompassing solution for Burn-out, Maslach sees the main hope of alleviating the problem in restructuring the work environment so as to relieve the emotional pressure on staff members. One way of doing this would be to rotate responsibilities so that the individual could alternate between work intensely involved with clients and lighter administrative tasks. Maslach also proposes reorienting the helper–client relationship in the human services so as to clarify mutual expectations and allow clients to assume greater responsibility.

It is likely that such changes will come about increasingly in the coming years, perhaps over the next generation, as public and private institutions become more aware of the costs of Burn-out. We do not stress them here, however, for two reasons. First, desirable as these changes might be, most of the people reading this book (including managers as well as staff members) will not be able to do much in the way of bringing them about now. Saying "It would be nice if the organization did such-and-such," or "Clients should . . ." won't help the individual worker do what he or she needs to do. Second (as Maslach and other observers are well aware), no matter how much the work environment is modified, some of the deepest causes of Burn-out cannot be altered. It is beyond the power of the most well-intentioned administrators to do away with clients' resistance to change, the scarcity of funds for human services, the tendency of people living in our society to engage in bureaucratic and political manipulation, and (probably most important) the profound frustration of being unable to exert as much influence on the world as one would wish. No intervention can do away with the pain and suffering that make the helping professions necessary while sometimes defeating their best efforts. As Sheldon Kopp[2] has emphasized, there is no magic. We just have to live with these situations.

Thus, intervention is considered here within the framework of psychiatrist William Glasser's Reality Therapy, an approach to rehabilitation and self-rehabilitation which holds that people must learn (with the help of supportive relationships) to accept reality and take responsibility for making choices that fulfill their needs. A person needs to accept the "givens" of the job, make a value judgment, and act. From this perspective many types of interventions become possible. All of them though, come with a tag that reads, "no guarantees."

With that cautionary note, there is a wide range of on-the-job as well as off-the-job interventions that we can consider. Although we are dealing with dissatisfactions that originate in the work situation, some of the most crucial interventions take place off-hours. These have to do with building a satisfying personal, social, or family life. If the job cannot be counted on to give complete satisfaction, then the job cannot be a person's only source of satisfaction.

Before turning to the interventions that may do some good, however, let's look first at some common interventions for Burn-out that *do not* work and see why they do not work.

FALSE INTERVENTIONS

False interventions are like a medical treatment that temporarily relieves the symptoms of a disease without altering its natural course. They address the surface aspects of a problem, but do not take into account what the problem really is and what steps are needed to bring about desired change. Unfortunately, false cures for Burn-out are being handed out all over. Typical of these are the "workshop high," legitimated malingering, and ill-considered job changes.

The "Workshop High"

These days the automatic solution to any problem in an organization is to run a workshop. When personnel in a state agency become lethargic, disgruntled, or simply "stale" from endless repetition of the daily routine, the state takes them off the job for a day, a weekend, or a week and pays them to attend a workshop given by an outside consultant (whose fee and living expenses are also paid by the state). The agency administrators are not unaware of what they are spending to give the staff this experience—an unavowed short-term intervention designed to lift sagging spirits under the guise of a legitimate budgetary item such as "staff development" or "skill retraining." They believe that it is worth the outlay to show staff members that the agency cares about them and to provide the agency with official verification that action has been taken.

But what exactly has happened? How much good has it done? When asked to describe the workshop three months later, a staff member might say, "It was fun meeting people there, and the guy they brought in to run it was really good." At the very least, the workshop was like a paid vacation. How much it improved services to clients, though, may not be very clear either to the staff or the administration. If what the participants did was mainly to "bitch" about their problems in the presence of a charismatic group leader, then the beneficial effects of the workshop on staff morale will have been short-term at best. It does make people feel good to discharge pent-up feelings. But when nothing really changes back on the job, after a while the workshop and the emotional release it has brought simply recede into the past.

Workshops can be a useful tool for learning, but they do not always have the intended results. A Naval officer who administers counseling programs at the national level has learned the futility of attending regional seminars with personnel over whom he has supervisory responsibility. Their emotional catharsis leaves him with more problems to solve. "If I go out there with a load on one shoulder," he says ruefully, "I come back with a load on both." He notes that people from the same base tend to keep to themselves at such gatherings, thus defeating the intended purpose. When staff members who work together every day go to an "outside" workshop and end up talking mainly with one another, the workshop becomes a glorified intra-agency "bitch session" of the sort described in Chapter 4.

On the other hand, suppose one attends a weekend workshop where one does mingle with new people and gains fresh perspectives. At the workshop one learns all sorts of ways in which one's organization could do a better job, if only everyone worked together to make the necessary changes. One comes back Monday morning all charged up to put the new ideas into practice, only to find that no one is interested. For everyone else, it's business as usual. As a disgruntled state employee put it, "You go to a workshop, you pop the cork, and nothing happens." The problem with workshops like the one just mentioned is that they leave the impression that individual good intentions can bring about organizational change, and that organizational change is a prerequisite for individual change. By putting things on an "if only" basis, they deflect responsibility from the individual to the organization. In this case, the workshop leader would have done better to make clear that, although one is not responsible for what the organization does, one is responsible for one's own actions (including working for constructive change if one so desires) and reactions (including disappointment if these efforts prove unsuccessful).

Now that Burn-out is becoming a household work in the helping professions, numerous individuals and organizations are conducting Burn-out workshops. Many of these are sound and useful programs. The authors are offering workshops on Burn-out in conjunction with this book. It is essential, though, for anyone running such a workshop to structure it so that participants can carry away more than a temporary "high," and for participants to come to the workshop with that goal in mind.

To draw an analogy with individual psychotherapy, social psychologist Stanton Peele[3] makes a crucial distinction between being in therapy for the sake of the experience of therapy itself and being in therapy for the sake of achieving certain desired ends in one's life outside of therapy. If therapy sessions make a person feel good without bringing about changes in the person's life, then the therapy is purposeless; it is an addiction. As Glasser puts in it *Reality Therapy,* [4]

> The therapist who accepts excuses, ignores reality, or allows the patient to blame his present unhappiness on a parent or on an emotional disturbance can usually make his patient feel good temporarily at the price of evading responsibility. He is only giving the patient "psychiatric kicks," which are no different from the brief kicks he may have obtained from alcohol, pills, or sympathetic friends before consulting the psychiatrist. When they fade, as they soon must, the patient with good reason becomes disillusioned with psychiatry.

Or else keeps going back to the therapist for a weekly "fix." The same is true for Burn-out workshops that allow workers to blame their difficulties on clients or the institution. When the "workshop high" fades, one is left either disillusioned or suspended in midair, waiting for the next workshop.

Legitimated Malingering

An effective Burn-out prevention program in a human service agency has many facets. These typically include Burn-out awareness training, in-service education to develop career skills and allow for increased responsibilities, outside educational opportunities, and rotation between client service and less stressful duties. Among the options that may be included in such a program is flexible scheduling that ensures a person enough time off to balance the commitment to work with a full personal life. For example, in a hospital where the social work staff is on call twenty-four hours a day, seven days a week, the supervisor of counselors may be authorized to give each employee a morning or afternoon off per week in return for night and weekend availability.

Unfortunately, this type of arrangement can be so appealing to both workers and supervisors that it is sometimes used indiscriminately. What is legitimate and constructive in one context may be an ill-considered panacea in another. The difference becomes clear when we list the aspects of our model hospital program that make the "time off" solution something other than a surreptitious expedient. (1) The time off is made up. A counselor who is on call for a weekend may get no calls or thirty. Although the number of hours the counselor may contribute varies, the fact that he or she is available during some off-duty hours and actually does put in some extra time means that the institution is getting something in return for waiving the standard forty-hour work week. Thus, the program can be justified on budgetary grounds. The counselor is not being given time off at the expense of clients and of the stockholders or taxpayers. (2) The policy applies consistently and equitably to all eligible employees. If counselors are given half a day off per week, so are nurses, orderlies, physical therapists, and dieticians—provided that they qualify by being on call for emergency duty. (3) The flexible scheduling is part of a coordinated program for dealing with Burn-out on many levels. It is not simply a stopgap intervention for chronically discontented workers. The various educational programs provided by the hospital ensure that the institution is not relying on time off alone as a solution to Burn-out (which it cannot be). Rather, the hospital is simultaneously implementing other, more lasting ways of increasing productivity and fostering personal growth. (4) The most important distinction follows from the other three: The program is conducted in an avowed, above-board manner. Since the employees in question are not getting a "break" at the expense of clients, the institution, other employees, or their own personal and professional development, there is nothing to hide. The supervisor of counselors can explain what he is doing to the hospital administrator, who in turn can give his approval because he knows that he has good grounds for defending this decision to the hospital's board of directors.

It is when the "time off" policy is not implemented in such defensible ways—when the time is not made up, when other employees are not given the same benefits, when there is no followup in other areas of Burn-out prevention—that it tends to be conducted surreptitiously, i.e., by a secret arrangement between the worker and supervisor. Even when the policy *is* framed in a justifiable manner, it may be more problematic to adopt such a policy in a public-sector institution, which is responsible not to individual or corporate owners but to the entire community. The board of directors of a private hospital may be prepared to listen to reasoned arguments from the hospital administrator. State officials, on the other hand, may not be so reasonable when they face the threat of out-of-context journalistic exposés of alleged abuses in public institutions ("State Hospital Gives Workers Time Off at Taxpayers' Expense"). Thus, it may not be possible to carry out even a well-planned Burn-out program openly in a publicly funded institution when it contains the potentially controversial shortened work week.

For whatever reason, when such a program cannot be carried out openly, it is better not to carry it out at all. When workers are given benefits covertly, the benefits can become a source of personal power for the supervisor who grants them. When time off is a favor given to the worker by the supervisor —rather than an officially sanctioned benefit that the worker enjoys as a matter of stated policy—the supervisor can ask for favors in return (or expect them without asking). This manipulative exploitation of what in other contexts is legitimate policy might be given the name "legitimated malingering." It is illustrated by the following case.

Arlene H. is a 22-year-old welfare caseworker without formal training who was hired by the state after graduating from college. Overwhelmed by her heavy caseload, she attended a summer workshop where she learned that "a caseworker should not have to work more than two days in a row." The head of the district office of the Welfare Department obligingly gave her Wednesday afternoons off to go swimming. Through this consideration her supervisor has won Arlene's gratitude and lifted her morale for the time being. If, however, the special arrangement between them were to come to the attention of the Director of Social Services for the state, we might imagine her having an exchange like this with Arlene's supervisor:

> Director of Social Services (DSS): Isn't this a bit irregular, giving someone time off with pay? What are your reasons for making an exception in this case?
>
> Welfare Administrator (WA): The job of a caseworker is an almost impossibly taxing one. As you know, we can't afford to hire enough caseworkers to serve all the families on welfare in this community. The ones we do have are so overworked that they quickly become discouraged and cease to function effectively. I'm being flexible with Arlene to keep her on the job and keep her happy. If she feels that the Department is listening to her and is considerate of her needs, she's going to work that much harder. In fact, I find her more highly motivated and

performing at a higher level since I've channeled all her malingering, so to speak, into that one afternoon per week.

DSS: You certainly have a point there. The head of the
Department of Corrections has told me the same thing regarding
prison guards. We're about as shorthanded with state police as
we are with caseworkers. My secretary just complained about
how overworked *she* was. She asked me for Friday mornings off
to go shopping. My response was, "Certainly, if you'll take a pay
cut of 10%." Now if Ms. H. wants to take off Wednesday afternoons and make up the time on weekends, that's fine. Otherwise,
if her workload is going to be reduced by 10%, we'll have to cut
her pay by 10%.

WA: You don't believe, then, that people who work directly with recipients of state services are especially overtaxed
and might deserve special consideration?

DSS: I know that people working in direct services are
under a lot of pressure. But there is no way I can convince the
Governor and the Legislature that welfare caseworkers are more
deserving of a break than psychiatric aides. There is no way I can
justify a 10% reduction in productivity for certain kinds of
personnel. If Ms. H. cannot do five days' work for five days' pay
like everyone else, then I wish her luck, and we'll put an ad in
the paper for a caseworker.

WA: I'll be happy to proceed on that basis, but I believe
we'll go on suffering the consequences in the form of turnover.
The problem isn't limited to Arlene H. We can put an ad in the
paper and get a dedicated, enthusiastic person with more training than Arlene has had, and we may lose that person, too, in
six months to a year. Then we'll have to break somebody in all
over again. I was suggesting that we might consider whether the
dollars-and-cents cost of some legitimated malingering might
not be less than the cost of turnover. Strictly off the record, we
may be able to run this agency more efficiently and get more
performance per dollar if we quietly accept things that, if they
were publicly known, would go against the values of the people
who are footing the bill. I know Joe Taxpayer thinks everybody
should spend every minute on the job working, but isn't it our
job to give Joe a better welfare agency by whatever means necessary?

DSS: I don't know what "our" job is, but I'm the one who
is responsible to the Governor, and through him to Joe Taxpayer. I have to make decisions that I can stand behind. I am
responsible for numerous agencies. Counselors, social workers,

medical and legal personnel—they're all under pressure. *I'm* under pressure. I'd like to go swimming, too. So at this juncture I'm not prepared to engage in any surreptitious administrative footwork to allow Ms. H. to swim on agency time.

In fact, the Director of Social Services may be going swimming during work hours, but she is not going to say so. "Surreptitious" practices really have to be surreptitious. Arrangements like the one between Arlene H. and the welfare agency head are quietly tolerated in many organizations, but because they do violate the explicit principles of the institution (and of the people who pay the bills, whether through private or public channels), they must be maintained informally. In this case, the Director of Social Services could not put herself in the position of giving Arlene's supervisor her explicit approval. If she did accept the idea that Arlene deserved a special break, it would have to be arranged in such a way that, at least officially, she would not know about it.

What are the benefits and costs of such "under the table" administration? An administrator needs to keep workers reasonably contented in their jobs, and one way to do it is by giving them ways to cut corners. Intentionally or not, the local agency head gains in Arlene a loyal subordinate who will keep his department productive within the overall agency. Small favors elicit large loyalties, which the administrator can draw upon for his own and the organization's benefit. What the organization loses is any possibility that Arlene might speak up and go against her supervisor when she believes him to be wrong.

It is Arlene herself who incurs the greatest costs. Her position is compromised. Dependent upon her supervisor's good will, she is not free to oppose him for fear of losing privileges. She is not likely to consider the option of leaving and taking another job where her boss will not be so friendly. She is stuck, and she knows it. Like the "drug-free" addiction counselors who are not held responsible for their actions on the grounds that they are "quasi-patients," she is being patronized as she is being protected. It must affect her self-esteem.

Furthermore, what happens when Arlene starts feeling

worn out and discouraged at four and a half days a week? The trouble with stopgap interventions—those that do not help a person learn to meet his or her needs—is that they do not solve any problems in the long run. Like the "workshop high," palliative remedies do not have lasting effects. They wear off. Again, the analogy of addiction[5] is illuminating. A person who is addicted to a drug lives in a small world where reality is altered so as to be unthreatening. In Arlene's case reality is being manipulated by administrative action rather than by a drug. It is in the nature of addiction that a person needs progressively larger doses of the drug (or other insulation from reality) to get from it the same satisfying sense of well-being. Addiction is not a stable condition, but a downward cycle of growing incapacity and guilt. What will happen to Arlene when having a half day off no longer does anything for her? Will her supervisor put her on a four-day week? What is the next patchwork solution? When does a sympathetic administrator run out of interventions?

A more productive intervention for Arlene would be to form a union with other counselors and present the case for better working conditions to the hospital administration. If successful, the counselors would be working with management to make legitimate policy changes. If unsuccessful, they would at least be confronting reality and testing its limits.

An intervention that at first sight looks like the one proposed for Arlene, but that actually is a more viable one, is one that Christine S. has devised for herself as a welfare caseworker. Christine spends many of her working hours away from her desk doing field work with clients. Every few weeks her field work takes her to the beach, where she spends a sunny afternoon forgetting her workday cares. She manages this by keeping up to date on her actual field work, some of it during what would not normally be working hours. At the same time, she is prepared to accept the consequences should she be discovered violating the formal requirements of the job. If she gets caught, she may or may not be able to defend herself by showing that she is fulfilling all her work requirements. But she knows that she cannot defend herself, for example, by claiming that this book says that it is "okay" to take time off as she does. She is taking the risk and the responsibility. Instead of having her boss "cover" for her, she is covering for herself. Unlike Arlene, she is not placing herself in a weakened position either psychologically or within the politics of her agency.

Changing Jobs—but Nothing Else

Changing jobs without changing one's own attitude and approach to the job is another superficial, stopgap remedy that can lead to a new cycle of disillusionment. An example is the case of Lynn M. in Chapter 9. When Lynn switched over from welfare to child abuse services, she did so simply because she was tired of the one job and wanted to try something else. *Anything* else had to be better, she thought. Occasionally it is better, but more often the unexpected problems in the new job balance out the known problems in the old.

There is, however, an initial burst of enthusiasm that comes with taking a new job. Some people feel such a strong need for this periodic "high" (a distant cousin of the "workshop high") that they change jobs frequently, moving on each time the "high" fades and the complications begin. In public as well as private agencies, there are highly mobile executives who, lacking personal ties in any of the areas where they work, throw themselves wholeheartedly into one job after another. Coming in with all the glamor of the "outsider" hired to "shake things up," they create as much excitement for the agency as for themselves. Organizations frequently seek this sort of person to touch off a spark of enthusiasm in their existing staff.

For the individual worker, this artificially revived enthusiasm masks a habit of running away from unfinished business. It can create difficulties at the organizational level as well. Although any agency needs a certain amount of turnover so that it can benefit from the newcomers' energy and fresh perspectives, an organization that takes its direction from enthusiastic transients may find that it has no direction at all. Just as people who move around from state to state tend to vote Democratic or Republican on the basis of national issues, without having much concern about the quality of the local officials they help elect, so the perpetual-motion enthusiast does not stay on the job long enough to identify with the program and feel its frustrations as his or her own. Hired to clean up one mess, the "whiz kid" as often as not leaves another mess behind. And the staff members who stay on are left with another reason to feel burned out.

False Hope and a Difficult Truth

What all false interventions for Burn-out have in common is the premise that a person can deal with Burn-out once and for all by one simple expedient. All of them attempt to get around the everpresent reality of Burn-out as something that a person must always be aware of and be dealing with. Burn-out is not like a special disease that one can "lick" with a shot of penicillin. Coping with it is more like keeping up a good everyday state of health by diet, rest, and exercise. That is, it is an ongoing process, as much a process of prevention and constant adjustment as of cure. False interventions for Burn-out are characterized by the hope of total regeneration, together with the reality of little or no lasting effect. True interventions involve the recognition that change is never final, together with the reality of some lasting progress. The person who deals realistically and successfully with Burn-out is like the addict or alcoholic who creates what amounts to a new life by taking things "one day at a time."

APPLYING REALITY THERAPY TO BURN-OUT

Although Reality Therapy does not give specific "answers" to the problems that lead to Burn-out, it does provide a framework within which such problems can be effectively confronted. Reality Therapy holds that one is individually responsible for doing what is necessary to fulfill one's needs (needs for self-worth, recognition, and so forth) within the "givens" of reality. This is not to deny that conditions on the job may really be bad and that one did not create those conditions. One is not responsible for the way things are or for what happened in the past. But one is responsible for accepting reality and doing something about it *now.*

When reality is discouraging, as it often is for people who are trying to help others, the easiest thing to do in the short run, as we saw in Chapter 4, is to "bitch" about it. But complaining does not solve any problems. There is a better, more productive response, and that is to make a value judgment.[6] One can ask oneself, "Is what I am doing what I really want to be doing? Is it helping to fulfill my needs? Given that these are the conditions of the job, do I want to be working at this kind of job? Is there a way I can handle the job so as to make it more satisfying? Is there any way to change things?"

As applied to Burn-out, the principles of Reality Therapy can be summed up in a few simple statements:

Accept the givens:

1. Understand them.
2. Live with them.
3. Work with them.

Living with the "givens" means accepting reality as the basis of one's actions, the starting point of whatever one decides to do. It means not letting one's hopes and desires take one's eyes off what actually is the case. Working with the "givens" means doing something about them. A starting point is not the same thing as an end point. Once one has accepted reality, one can work to change those parts of it over which one has some control.

These principles will be elaborated in this chapter and applied in the next chapter to problem-solving on the job and life expansion off the job. First, however, we will introduce

another therapeutic model that can serve as a useful comple-
ment to Reality Therapy.

Rational-Emotive Therapy

Psychologist Albert Ellis[7] has catalogued countless variations of the "musts," "shoulds," and "if onlys" of wishful and
self-punishing thinking in an analysis that shows how faulty
thinking keeps people from facing reality. Ellis's Rational-Emotive Therapy is based on the premise that most emotional dis-
turbances can be traced to certain common irrational ideas.
Here are some of these ideas as they apply to Burn-out in the
helping professions:

1. The idea that it is a dire necessity for a helping professional to be loved or appreciated by every client.
2. The idea that one must always enjoy the favor of one's
   supervisor.
3. The idea that one must be thoroughly competent and
   successful in doing one's job if one is to consider oneself worthwhile.
4. The idea that anyone who disagrees with one's own
   ideas and methods is "bad" and becomes an opponent
   to be scorned, rejected, or anathematized.
5. The idea that one should become very upset over clients' problems and failings.
6. The idea that it is awful and catastrophic when clients
   and the institution do not behave as one would like
   them to.
7. The idea that one's unhappiness is caused by clients or
   the institution and that one has little or no ability to
   control one's emotional reactions.
8. The idea that until clients and the institution
   straighten themselves out and do what is right one has
   no responsibility to do what is right oneself.
9. The idea that there is invariably a right, precise, and
   perfect solution to human problems and that it is catastrophic if that solution is not found.

We can make up a statement of this sort for every item on the 12-point planning board—low pay, powerlessness, bad office politics, and all the rest. "If only I didn't have to work such long hours. . . ." "If only I didn't have so much paperwork. . . ." "If only I had more training. . . ." "If only my decisions counted for something. . . ." "If only I could see the results of my labors. . . ." In each case the irrational response is to assume that things *have* to be the way one thinks they "should" be before one can act constructively or gain satisfaction from one's work. The rational response is to take what's there and see what one can do with it (or else consider the option of leaving the job).

For those who recognize some of their own irrational beliefs among those listed (and who does not, at one time or another?), Rational-Emotive Therapy offers a step-by-step procedure for analyzing and redirecting one's thinking. Here is an example:

A. ACTIVATING EXPERIENCE: A man whom one is counseling has started beating his wife again.

B. IRRATIONAL BELIEF OR INTERPRETATION: "It's my fault. If I were a good counselor, he wouldn't be beating his wife. If I can't stop him from doing it, my effectiveness as a counselor will be called into question." and/or "He really is hopeless, isn't he? A bad apple from the word go. They really do stick me with the losers."

C. UPSETTING EMOTIONAL CONSEQUENCES: One loses a night's sleep worrying about the case and begins to feel run-down.

D. DISPUTING OF IRRATIONAL IDEAS: "What makes me think that I have the power to stop someone from doing what I don't want him to do? Why should I be able to prevent bad things from happening? Why does one setback make me a bad counselor? And why does doing a bad thing make this man a bad person?"

E. COGNITIVE AND EMOTIONAL EFFECT: "Even if I were the best counselor in the world, I couldn't count on being able to stop this man from beating his wife. He has been and is subjected to many influences on his behavior besides myself. He is doing something bad now, but that does not mean that he will always do it. It makes him a fallible, not a bad, person. Because he is doing something bad, though, it is my responsibility to do everything that is reasonably within my power to stop him."

This self-questioning technique enables one to put into practice the principles of Rational-Emotive Therapy by exposing and correcting the irrational presuppositions that influence one's feelings and actions. It can help one take responsibility for the choices one makes rather than blame one's own reactions on people and events that do not meet one's expectations.

Karen Horney[8] uses the expression "The tyranny of the should" in referring to the "neurotic claims" that helping professionals, like other human beings, sometimes make on reality. When a client makes an appointment with a counselor, the counselor can reasonably expect the client to keep the appointment. But if the reasonable expectation becomes an unquestioned expectation, an assumption of right, a *demand,* then the counselor is trying to control the client and at the same time giving the client control over his or her reactions. A counselor who starts thinking, "Why don't these fools appreciate what I'm doing for them?" is getting into the emotional stalemate that Horney analyzes and that Ellis's methods offer a way out of.

TAKING RESPONSIBILITY

Nothing is more important in handling Burn-out than to know what responsibilities one does and does not have. One is not responsible for clients or for the institution, but one is responsible for oneself. This does not mean that one does not become involved with clients or that one does not try to change the way the institution is run. It simply means that one is responsible for one's own actions, not theirs, and that one remains responsible for one's actions regardless of what they do or don't do.

The director of in-service training at a school for the mentally retarded says, "I always tell new personnel that for the first six months all they have to do is function and survive. Until that point they are not responsible for the school." What he means is that while they are learning the ropes they should not feel that they have to worry about influencing the way the school is run. That is wise counsel. But although participating in policy decision making may become one of their responsibilities, staff members are *never* responsible for the institution. The problem with thinking oneself responsible for the institution is that it makes one start thinking that the institution is responsible for oneself. When the institution does not respond to one's efforts to make it better, one may begin to let that affect one's own performance.

The same is true with clients. A helping professional (and this includes paraprofessionals, since one purpose of this discussion is to teach paraprofessionals professional skills and attitudes) cannot let the frustrating behavior of clients determine his or her own feelings and actions. As a helper one has a job to do, and one can best serve one's clients by recognizing that it remains one's responsibility to do that job regardless of the way clients respond.

Does this sound as if we are demanding an unrealistic perfection of helpers that we do not demand of clients? Professional responsibility is not the same thing as perfection. Paradoxically, the way a person generally achieves such professionalism is by cultivating a degree of detachment from clients. One is free to be responsible for oneself when one recognizes that every client is responsible for himself or herself. Detachment here does not mean indifference, callousness, or cynicism. People come into the helping fields because they care about people, and part of the helper's job *is* to care—to go on caring and not give up on a person even when the results seem most discouraging. One is best able to do this, however, when one is able to go home and get a good night's sleep, knowing that one has done a good day's work whether or not clients have responded. It is the helper's responsibility to help people change. Whether or not people actually change is their responsibility.

We are, of course, returning here to the issue of overidentification, which was discussed in Chapter 3. Coping with the tendency to overidentify is a matter of limiting one's commitment as a person (limiting the commitment of one's own emotions) without limiting one's commitment as a professional help-giver. This is not an easy recipe to follow. How does one sort out one's emotions? Here is how some individuals have done it:

1. A psychiatric aide: "While I'm trying to help people change I need to remind myself to leave them some space not to change."

2. The Director of Nursing at a hospital: "I used to be on call all the time, as if no one could ever do without me. Then I came to realize that I'm not indispensable. I may like to think I am, but if I were to die tomorrow the hospital and patients would go on quite well without me."

3. An alcoholism counselor: "People who want everything done for them have to learn to help themselves."

4. A family counselor: "I used to take calls at all hours of the day or night. Now I put on my answering machine when I don't want to be disturbed. I think it's better for clients to know that sometimes they'll have to wait. That way they don't become dependent on immediate rescue."

5. An ex-priest who has worked in various secular helping roles: "Previously I thought I was obligated to serve. Now, I simply offer. If people want it, fine. If

not, fine. I'm not laying anything on them, and they're not laying frustration on me. If I'm frustrated, it's my frustration."

6. A psychiatric social worker: "I used to be wiped out all the time because I thought I had no choice about letting people into my space. I see now that it's my decision when to let people into my space. I'm learning to say no."

7. An educational policy planner with the federal government: "I want to create programs that will enable people to help themselves. I don't want to be a do-gooder giving out pity and condescension."

8. A nurse on a surgical unit: "When I was walking around that floor obviously pregnant, my patients showed me just how much they could do for themselves."

Although our prescription for allocating responsibility between helper and client is simple and straightforward, in practice it is a more delicate matter. Every individual has a different way of coming to terms with the emotional vulnerability that one displays as a beginner. That vulnerability has to be tempered, but not completely lost. Experiences like the following are common for a person just coming into the field: One overidentifies with a client only to find that the client is manipulating one's emotional involvement. So one overreacts by saying to oneself, "I *will not* be manipulated! I will make sure that no one is going to manipulate me today!" Of course, one cannot work with people if one puts up that kind of defense. Manipulation is something that goes on between people all the time. Nowhere does it go on more than in the helping professions. It is one of the "givens."

How much does one give of oneself? How much does one hold back? In any situation one has to strike a balance that depends on how one feels, how the client feels, and what seems right to both parties. Where that balance falls will vary from day to day. The degree of availability that will help the client without burning out the helper will emerge from the nature of the involvement the helper has with the client—not the amount of time the two of them spend together, but the depth and potency of the connection. Reaching that depth is something that no amount of training and nothing said in this book can prepare one for. It comes with experience.

REALISTIC EXPECTATIONS

Developing realistic expectations comes under the heading of "living with the 'givens.' " It is not a matter of what one does so much as how one interprets its meaning: what standards one measures oneself against, what one thinks one can accomplish, what one sees as success and failure. The more one's expectations are in line with reality, the less frustration one will suffer.

There are certain things that anyone going into the helping fields can expect. To begin with, one can expect to see many of the problems discussed in this book. As a result, one can expect to go through a Burn-out process of greater or lesser severity. It is one of the "givens." It is bound to happen, so one may as well be prepared for it, live with it, and use it to advantage by coming up with creative solutions.

Expect to be doing a difficult job without sufficient resources or outward rewards. Expect to have to get along with some disagreeable people and to have to show tolerance for outrageous viewpoints. Expect to be unable to do any of these things all the time. Expect to be far from perfect, and expect clients and colleagues to be far from perfect.

Reality Therapy teaches people not to be hypercritical, not to judge themselves and others by an unrealistic standard of perfection. Sidney Simon uses the term "red-pencil mentality" to refer to the tendency to focus on occasional mistakes while forgetting all the things one is doing right. Realistic expectations begin at home. Or, as a clinical psychologist puts it, "It was by being realistic about myself that I learned to be realistic about what a patient could do."

Measuring Success

A primary contributor to Burn-out is the difficulty helpers have in evaluating the results of their efforts. How does one know when one is doing any good? In the absence of clearcut criteria, the red-pencil mentality comes into play in at least two important ways: (1) the expectation that every case show progress; (2) the reliance on recidivism rates as the only available "concrete" measure of success. Whether the issue at hand is alcoholism, drug addiction, criminal behavior, psychiatric disabilities, or behavioral or learning disorders in children, helping professionals and paraprofessionals tend to regard each relapse on the part of the client as a reflection on the counselor. Where clients typically relapse one or more times, life becomes frustrating for the person who is trying to help.

By having other measures of success whereby the cards are not so thoroughly stacked against one, one can take a big step toward alleviating the problem of Burn-out. In speaking with many individuals in various fields who have successfully coped with unpromising prognoses and poor success rates, we have come up with a number of alternative ways of interpreting progress that yield both a brighter and more realistic picture.

1. *Set Realistic Goals.* As Albert Ellis would say, one is bound to be disappointed if one starts out thinking one can, should, or has to save the world. Defining one's goals as precisely as possible helps one keep one's expectations from getting out of hand by staying attuned to what is possible as well as to the mission and job requirements of one's agency.

In Chapter 9 we looked into the case of Lynn M., a social worker who ran up against frustration in welfare and child abuse services. One of her frustrations was that although she could sometimes stop people from physically abusing their children, she did not have the time (or the power) to help people reach a deeper understanding of their family relationships. Lynn's feeling that her efforts were superficial and incomplete is understandable, but it may well be that the mandate and the budget of the child abuse agency did not allow for going beyond the problem the agency was explicitly created to deal with. Stopping the beatings was the job at hand, and people who needed additional counseling could be referred elsewhere.

In a similar vein, counselors in drug rehabilitation clinics often find it frustrating that so much emphasis is placed on detoxification rather than long-term counseling to help addicts recreate their lives on a drug-free basis. Again, one has to ask what the goal of the program is. Given the budgetary and staffing problems of most drug clinics, just helping people become drug-free at all may be a sufficiently ambitious goal. Once they have detoxed, addicts have an opportunity to reexamine their lives and become more productive. Some of them do in fact make use of that opportunity. Perhaps that is all one can hope for. In any case, the appropriate intervention for a discontented counselor is not to expect the director and city council to expand the mandate of the program, but to make a value judgment about whether it is sufficiently rewarding to work under the given limitations.

A psychiatrist who has run several drug and alcohol programs has dealt with his own susceptibility to Burn-out by learning to define success in terms of more modest goals than total recovery for the addict or the alcoholic. The occasional complete recoveries are inspiring. Nonetheless, longer periods of abstinence, fewer and less severe relapses, less destructive physical and emotional effects, and an improved ability to function in society may be useful results of therapy for the individual, family, and community. Such partial successes are real successes and should be incorporated into a helper's goals.

2. *Focus on the Successes, not the Failures.*   No one can help everybody. That fact of life is embodied in the principle of *triage,* which was discussed in Chapter 1. One must allocate one's time and energy and make one's major efforts where they are likely to do the most good—not with the people who can make it without much help, not with the people who probably are not going to make it regardless, but with the people who look as if they could benefit from a decisive intervention. An alcoholism counselor who has learned this lesson describes her implementation of triage:

> There are some cases I'll put a lot of energy into. For instance, a young woman who wanted to get sober but could not go into a hospital because she had a child to take care of came to me for help. There were many signs that she was well motivated. She had thrown out all the liquor in her house, had invited her mother to stay and support her, and was willing to accept a referral to A.A. I worked out a treatment plan with her, including contingency plans if she got into trouble, and asked her to check in with me every day. She is doing that and has remained sober.
>
> Now here is an example of the kind of case I do not put much energy into. A man who always comes in drunk and who by his own admission has been in "every hospital up and down the East coast" for alcoholism came in and asked me to put him in the hospital. I told him, "You know where the hospital is. You know how to get in there. If you want to work with me this time and really get sober, I'll work with you. But if you just want to dry out you can go to the hospital yourself." If this had been one of my first cases I would have called the hospital, arranged his admission, taken him in my car, spoken with the staff, and made the same elaborate plans I made for the woman who really wanted help. But not anymore.

The same realism that dictates the use of triage criteria before the fact should be applied in evaluating success ratios after the fact. Failure and recidivism are part of the job in the helping professions. No one in the field can afford to be fully invested in the outcome of every single case. Each individual needs to arrive at a rough idea of what proportion of successes makes the job worthwhile. That proportion does not have to be large. A family services caseworker, for example, says, "Out of every twenty clients I'd say I really reach one. But to me that's encouraging." For her, an occasional breakthrough validates the overall experience of trying to help people.

Paying selective attention to the good outcomes is a biased way to look at things, but it makes sense. It's a lot better than the "red-pencil" bias of looking at the failures and not the successes. The family services caseworker is looking at the one case in 20 where her presence and her actions have made a difference. The other 19 would not suddenly be resolved and disappear if she left the field. Those problem areas would still be there, with or without her. It is not as if she has one win and 19 defeats, but one win, period. She has accomplished something, and if that is enough to keep her going, more power to her.

Carefully defining goals and paying attention to small gains and partial successes are sound practices for everyone from the paraprofessional counselor to the top administrator. At the higher managerial levels, where it is just as unlikely that all goals will be achieved as that none will, it is especially useful to itemize priorities. To take one example, the director of a comprehensive community alcoholism program originally had intended to create a multimodality program offering all the services that were otherwise unavailable in that community. A few years later, reviewing the progress made to date, he could say that the counseling and education programs had developed quite satisfactorily and that detox was being handled in conjunction with a local hospital. On the minus side, the outreach and supervised residence programs that he had hoped to develop had not gotten off the ground. By conceiving of his larger goal as a composite of several lesser goals, he was able to make a discriminating assessment of his accomplishment and gain satisfaction from what had been done.

3. *Focus on the Process, not the Result.*   There is a great deal more to helping people than seeing the cures and recoveries at the end of the tunnel. There is the exercise of skills, the human contact, the emotional involvement, the development of a rapport and a dialogue with clients, and the pleasure of doing an important job well. As with any art, the "doing" is as important as the "done." Experienced helpers who continue to gain satisfaction from their work despite all obstacles understand that they cannot depend on results which are beyond their control to justify their efforts. The satisfaction they get comes in great part from being out there working with people and carrying out their own side of the relationship with sensitivity and skill.

Part of the process that should not be overlooked is the personal benefits one gains from working in the field —benefits that may range from emotional maturation to qualification for further training and career advancement. This is a delicate issue to deal with, since self-serving motives can easily undermine the primary goal of helping others. But self-effacement is no more healthy than self-aggrandizement; as in any other field, a balance has to be struck between personal needs and a commitment to ideals. If, for example, the increased self-understanding one gains from being a psychologist, counselor, or social worker makes the experience worthwhile and keeps one from burning out even when one cannot help many clients, that's all to the good.

4. *Keep a Time Perspective.*   Besides expecting good results in every case, another error of the novice is to expect results right away. With experience the helping professional develops a more realistic time frame for

interpreting progress with a particular type of client. A counselor who works with female adolescent delinquents reports, "I used to expect immediate change, but it takes three to six months for any progress to appear, and sometimes the girls don't stay around that long." A psychiatric social worker who works in prisons and hospitals says, "I'm beginning to get some long-range feedback. A person I've seen may call me up six months later and tell me, 'I hated your guts then, but what you told me made a difference.' "

Where long-term psychotherapy is involved, of course, it may be a question of years rather than months. A psychologist who has faced the frustration of seeing individuals go on and on in therapy with no progress (or else with a cycle of progress and regression) has had to "remind myself intellectually that people reach plateaus of growth, and that they have to stay at each plateau for some time to consolidate that phase of their growth." Such patience can have its rewards. A psychologist or psychiatrist who sees addicts or alcoholics through a complete recovery process lasting two or three years will, on the basis of that experience, have a more realistic idea of what such clients can do if given only a short time. From that perspective, merely detoxifying in a period of weeks may be seen as substantial progress.

5. *Do not Interpret Results Self-Referentially.*   If one is going to help others while maintaining a healthy emotional balance, one will need to keep one's own efforts in perspective when evaluating both good and bad outcomes. As a counselor remarked, "I didn't get people sick, and I'm not going to be the one to get them well." Not only that, but sometimes one does not even know when one does play an important role in getting someone well. One will not often be lucky enough to get a phone call from an ex-client saying, "You really made the difference for me six months ago."

Enthusiastic converts to sobriety or the "straight" life sometimes have to remind themselves how many hospitalizations, how many arrests, how many counseling sessions it took even to begin to make an impression on them. Who can say which one had the decisive effect? A prison inmate may hear a heartfelt lecture from a counselor and pay no attention. Years later, when he is at a critical point in his life, he may recall that message and finally assimilate it so that it begins to influence his actions. By then, however, he may have moved to a different part of the country, where other counselors will harvest the seeds that the first counselor planted. A counselor, then, may not have much to do with some of the miracles that he or she sees, yet may have a lot to do with some that he or she never sees.

Definitions of Success

No precepts can capture all the ways in which people learn to find meaning in their work. The definition of success is a highly individualized, subjective matter, as the following examples suggest:

"Success is when someone is a little happier, a little less angry, a little more disposed to say something meaningful to another person."

"I consider myself successful when I can stimulate people, wake them up, get them to think. I like to turn on that light bulb inside a person. After that I don't know what's going to happen."

"I don't compute success rates in the aggregate. I look at every person as an individual and consider how that person has changed in terms of his or her problems and needs."

"I don't have any fantasy that I can save every patient. I just want to see myself as doing some good some of the time."

"When you spend a year with a patient you know what a small change can mean. A woman who has been afraid to leave her house for a year gets into a taxi and comes to see a doctor. A man who's been assaultive is able to be with the other patients. Someone who's been sitting on a couch spouting stories finally gets up off the couch. The patient won't say anything, but you know that it's a step toward a normal life. Sometimes, though, the change comes so slowly that you need to have your peers call attention to it. A lot of the satisfaction on the job can only come from co-workers who believe in what you're doing. You won't get it from patients directly."

"We had a deaf patient who was put in the psychiatric hospital because his family didn't want to take responsibility for dealing with his disability. He was ridiculed, pushed around, treated like an animal. It seemed that nobody would ever give him a chance. Then a few of us on the staff took responsibility and got behind him. We got him using a hearing aid, and now he's leaving the hospital. That's satisfaction."

An Inoculation of Burn-Out

At the end of Chapter 9 we reviewed the four stages of Burn-out in the case of Lynn M., a welfare and child-abuse caseworker. Having reached the end of the line—apathy—in her second job as she had in her first, Lynn resigned and took a job in family services. Here she was assigned by the courts to counsel families involved in divorce proceedings and help make custody arrangements for children.

She had changed jobs once before without much effect, but this time was different. The job requirements were specific, clearly defined, and, she felt, feasible. Instead of being expected to take care of any problem that arose and provide any service that people requested, she could set limits on her own involvement and refer families to other agencies for additional help. Because she understood the "givens" when she took the job, she was not so likely to be disillusioned later.

Thus the job itself helped structure Lynn's expectations. But it was not only the job that had changed. Lynn's prior experiences had made her more realistic as well. She concedes that even this job would not have satisfied her in her initial stage of enthusiasm:

> When I was just out of college I wasn't looking for limits. No job would have met my needs then. I needed to feel needed and depended upon. I needed to feel I could change people's lives. My needs are different now. I don't have to do everything for people. I don't feel insulted if people don't call on me in a crisis. I've learned that I don't have the right to impose my values on others.

Lynn improved her situation by two simultaneous interventions —one of them objective (finding a better job) and one of them subjective (changing her attitude). She increased her satisfaction by redefining what satisfaction meant to her. Her changed expectations made it possible for her to bring about and take advantage of a better objective situation.

Ironically, Lynn feels that her present job is fulfilling some of the unmet expectations of her previous job. By working out appropriate living situations for children of divorced couples, she sees herself as doing more for children in the long run than when she was trying to stop child abuse after the fact. Her biggest problems on the job come in dealing with lawyers, who know all the "rules of the game" that families do not know. Every day she sees how much power lawyers have and, by contrast, how little power she has. Her response for the time being is to stay where she is and ride with what she thinks will be a favorable tide. As the role of the family relations officer expands beyond divorce proceedings to other legal issues, she expects to gain greater familiarity with the court system. Eventually she would like to go to law school and become "one of the new breed of attorneys specializing in family cases."

By exposing herself to two heavy doses of Burn-out (but not staying at those two jobs long enough to develop a case of chronic apathy), Lynn built up her defenses against later exposures. It is through this kind of "inoculation" that many people in the field become seasoned professionals, resistant to the effects of frustration. When Fred R., whose case also appeared in Chapter 9, came back into alcoholism counseling after burning out of drug counseling, he came back better prepared by experience as well as education. Enthusiastic as he again was, he now knew that alcoholics cannot be expected to become sober; he knew first-hand the dangers of the counseling environment for the recovering alcoholic or addict; and he knew that he could best deal with the inevitable failures and disappointments on the job if he did not think of the job as his whole life or as a permanent career. Although Fred was to relapse at least once more, his "shot" of Burn-out on the whole served him well.

What such an inoculation requires is not only experience, but an awareness of what the experience means. Lynn can serve as a model in having had the consciousness to interpret her experience to best advantage. With such understanding, constructive action becomes possible.

Chapter 11

PROBLEM-SOLVING ON AND OFF
THE JOB

This is the second half of our program for intervention, the active, "doing" part, that is, working with the "givens." Once one accepts reality, what can one do to make it better? It turns out that there are a number of things that can be done, both on and off the job. What one needs are techniques for discovering what these interventions are.

CONFRONTING THE SITUATION

More than knowledge, it takes energy and courage to confront existing conditions. The barriers to moving oneself off center are more emotional than intellectual. The following cases illustrate what it means and how it feels to get moving. Some of them have been mentioned in previous chapters; they are brought together here to highlight their common element, namely, a spirit of hopeful movement and constructive change.

Sybil E., a nurse, has been on the move professionally for years. Having worked in hospitals, physicians' offices, nursing homes, and as a teacher in nursing school, she is ready to act when she becomes dissatisfied or sees an opportunity to improve her position. When she gets frustrated, she does not just brood over it; she goes through want ads and university catalogues. As she explains, "The feeling that there is hope generates action, which generates more hope. Without hope things would get heavy. I have to believe that something can be done."

Margaret B., a high school teacher who resigned after suffering severe emotional trauma from a decade-long stalemate with unsympathetic colleagues and superiors, began to bounce back after two years' inactivity by leaving an unsupportive marriage and turning to the healing voices of art. "By listening to what I heard when I turned down the noise in my mind," she says, "I realized that there was no external system greater than my own internal system." She is now seeking a Ph.D. in educational psychology.

Sharon A., a social worker, originally went into family counseling, only to be rejected as "too aggressive" by a supervisor who found her energy threatening. She then took a job in addiction counseling, where, working with a dynamic supervisor, she found a congenial environment for her own drive and creativity. Still interested in family therapy, Sharon has had to adjust her expectations to what she regards as the narrower intellectual vistas of drug and alcohol rehabilitation. At the same time, she has expanded her job by enthusiastically taking on supervisory responsibilities.

Warren C., a counselor in the state corrections department, always resented his supervisor's "Mickeymouse" directives. Then he would say to himself, "Somebody has to do these things, and I guess I'm the one designated." Although accepting such disagreeable necessities, he began to test how much he could structure his own time within the limits of the job. For instance, he developed a course for inmates on social deviancy and taught it himself in addition to some courses at the community college. In this way he put into practice his own, more appealing job definition (one that involved more direct contact with inmates) as well as the official job definition.

Sandra K., a family counselor in training for her M.S.W., has frequently found herself frustrated by the indifference of supervisors and institutions. When that happens, she says, "I realize that change has to come from within myself, from my own strength." This strength has come partly from the fact that she is a mature woman with the experience of raising a family behind her, and partly from the fact that "at each stage I've had one person—say, a field placement supervisor—who has believed me and believed in me." With that support she has been able to take risks and keep her positive accomplishments in view even when rebuffed or attacked.

In the course of our interviews there have been two individuals who turned every problem on the 12-point planning board exercise into an opportunity, every negative statement into a positive one. Each of them interpreted every item as demonstrating why he had a good situation or why it was his own responsibility to make the situation better. One of these men, not surprisingly, is a psychiatrist. He remarked, "I create my own rewards. I've always created the situations I've wanted for myself, and I imagine I'll still be doing so ten years from now."

The other is Mark N., who eight years earlier was a heroin addict. After breaking in as a stereotypical jive-talking addiction counselor, he began to develop new expectations which "came from within, not from outside pressure." Seeking more knowledge and greater participation in the program, he formulated a concept of personal and professional responsibility which challenged and transcended the organizational hierarchy:

> The organization's limitations should never be allowed to get between the counselor and the client. What matters to the client is not the organizational structure, but the quality of the individ-

ual staff member. Professionalism is not three letters after your name; it's a moral and ethical approach to people, one that anyone can practice.

Mark practiced it to the extent that he became supervisor of counselors. In that post he insisted that counselors learn professional skills and saw to it that those who did were rewarded with commensurate responsibility. However, these initiatives and their successful implementation met with indifference from the agency administering the program. Mark, who at first was angry, now accepts this bureaucratic short-sightedness as one of the "givens." "You have to learn the system and adapt to it," he concludes. "You make changes where you can, as quietly as you can." Asked about his prospects over the next ten years, he says, "If I'm not where I want to be, it'll be my fault."

What do these people have in common? They combine a realism about the outside world with an audacious confidence in themselves. They try new things while paying close attention to feedback. They are continually adjusting their expectations, both upward (to the reality of their accomplishments) and downward (to the sometimes disappointing results).

Some recurrent themes run through these vignettes. One is Jerome Frank's[1] notion of the role of hope in positive change. Another is the idea of "inner strength." Some people, it is true, are better equpped by past experience to exercise their own strength than are others. But that is where Glasser's concept of the "transmission of strength" comes in. In several of these cases there is mention of a supportive individual such as a supervisor, teacher, experienced colleague, or family member who intervened at a crucial moment. Mark N. served as such a support for other counselors. It takes some risks to get out of a rut, and the strength needed to take risks is transmitted from one person to another in an involving relationship. Glasser stresses the importance of involvement—between therapist and client, trainer and trainee, supervisor and staff member—as giving a person the strength to accept and confront reality.

Offering supportive involvement is an essential part of the therapist's, trainer's, or supervisor's job.

A Problem-Solving Exercise

Having the strength to act is not the same as knowing what to do. Confronting reality means coming up with alternatives and choosing among them. In *Consider the Alternative,*[2] Lee Silverstein presents a method of doing this that also brings into play the support of others when the commitment to act is made. Here is the sequence of steps in this exercise as it might be presented to a group of helping professionals:

First, write down a seemingly insoluble work-related problem—any problem that you feel strongly as your own. For example, "One of my co-workers speaks to clients in a high-handed, patronizing way that lowers their self-esteem and undermines my efforts to help them."

Then just "brainstorm" and write down as many alternative solutions as you can think of. Do not try to evaluate any of them at this stage. You will not be able to think of many solutions if you let the "red-pencil mentality" edit them out before you get them down on paper.

When you've exhausted your brainstorming capacity, you can evaluate all the alternatives by putting each into one of the following categories:

1. Most Likely.   Other things being equal, what do you think will happen? Usually the answer is, "I'll go on complaining, and nothing will change."
2. Most Desirable.   This is the "magic wand" solution, where you can indulge in any fantasy. For example, "The offending party will disappear from the face of the earth."
3. Alternatives With More than a 50/50 Chance of Success.   An example here might be, "I'll write a memorandum to the director documenting my co-worker's unprofessional conduct."

4. Alternatives With Less than a 50/50 Chance of Success.   Here you might list some remedies that have been tried previously without success, such as, "I'll have a talk with my errant co-worker about the harm he/she is doing."

5. Least Desirable.   This might be, "I'll criticize my co-worker publicly, thus causing him/her to retaliate in such a way as to damage my professional reputation." Or "I'll give up on the situation and quit my job." Or it might simply be the same as the "most likely" solution: "I'll do nothing, and things will stay the same." One of the immediate benefits of this exercise, before a solution is even decided upon, is simply to show how often the thing that is going to happen anyway is about the worst thing that can happen. You do not know what the outcome will be if you try to do something about the problem. But you can be pretty sure of the outcome if you do nothing, namely, no change.

The next step is to decide on a plan of action by informally weighing the probable costs and benefits of each proposed solution. What is it likely to accomplish? How unpleasant will it be to carry out? Is it likely to have consequences that you want to avoid (e.g., making you lose your job)? This is where the value judgment comes in: "Do I want to do this? Is it worth it? What consequences am I willing to risk to have a chance at solving the problem?"

When you have chosen a course of action, make a commitment to act within a definite period of time. Ask yourself how soon you can expect to be able to put your plan into effect. If you choose "having a talk with my co-worker," you may not be sure that both of you will have the time open to talk Monday morning. Can you do it by Monday at 2 o'clock, then? Perhaps your co-worker will not come in Monday. Then how about Tuesday? If you choose "writing a critical memo to the director the next time my co-worker acts inappropriately," how soon do you expect that to happen? How about two weeks from now? The idea is to set a realistic time limit that allows for no excuses.

A commitment is really only a commitment if it is avowed publicly. That is why this exercise works especially well in groups. For one thing, another person might come up with a solution for someone who is too close to the situation to see it clearly. The major benefit, though, is the support one can enlist from others in holding oneself to one's commitment. The workshop leader might instruct group members to exchange phone numbers and arrange to call each other at specified times to see if they have followed through on their commitments. Of course, a person does not have to be in a formal group or workshop situation to do this; one can do it privately with a co-worker. One of the best outcomes a Burn-out workshop can have is for the staff members in an organization to form problem-solving groups that meet on a continuing basis.

The commitment to act, however, must be voluntary. It must result from a freely made value judgment, not group pressure. The group leader might say to a participant, "Would you like to call me collect at the time we've agreed upon and let me know whether you've followed through and what the outcome was? Does that seem to you to be worth doing?" In other words, one does not make someone else's problem one's own. One cares because that person cares. If the person does not care, there's nothing one can do—except burn out from frustration. Using this exercise to confront problems contributing to Burn-out in the helper also provides a model for helping clients confront *their* problems. The helper cares because the client cares. That is the difference between involvement and overinvolvement.

Finally, the exercise does have one catch. If there is something one can do about the problem, and if one decides not to do it, one loses the right to complain. One has chosen (whether explicitly or through subsequent failure to carry out the plan of action) to go on living with the problem. No excuses, please.

JOB-RELATED INTERVENTIONS

Thus far we have accepted the "givens," decided to try to change things, enlisted the support of "significant others," and devised a method for finding possible solutions. But what solutions are there? Here are some typical on-the-job interventions for Burn-out. All of them can do some good when applied in the right place at the right time. All of them, however, come with a warning label. First, any intervention is more likely to work if it is carried out consciously and with a clear purpose rather than as a reflex reaction to dissatisfaction (though one can always be lucky). Second, there is no guarantee that any intervention will work. Uncertainty is one of the "givens." Third, beware of the cycle of enthusiastic expectations discussed in Chapter 3. A person who starts thinking, "If only I could get a better job. . . ." or "Now that I have my degree, it's clear sailing from here on," is leaving himself or herself open for the next cycle of disillusionment. New solutions create new problems—maybe not such bad ones as before, but even that is not certain. One cannot know all the "givens" of the new situation until one actually gets there.

Further Education

Going back to school is both an on- and off-the-job intervention. It takes place away from the job setting (a plus in itself), but it is usually undertaken at least in part to gain professional advancement. In our degree-conscious society it is about the most common and most consistently useful intervention available to the person who is at a "career dead end." As before, Roger F.'s career as a drug counselor nicely illustrates a broader phenomenon:

After the clinical conference at which the scribe put me in my place by leaving the room when I got up to speak, I went to the Medical Director and asked him to clarify something he had said to me six months before when he suspended me for having an affair with a woman client. "If a professional did this, we'd fire him," he had told me. "But you fellas are different." What he had meant, he explained, was this: "We expect you to act like our addict clients because that's what you are. Being a counselor is no career. We're just paying you so that for the time being you won't take drugs." But then he added, "I understand that you're going to school. Keep it up."

That speech made clear where I stood. It lit up both paths for me—the one going back to the streets and the one going forward. It told me that by taking some college courses I might be headed somewhere.

After that Roger accelerated his educational program until he left the drug clinic and went to school full time, eventually obtaining his B.A. and M.S.W. degrees. With those credentials he had a wide range of teaching, consulting, and direct service positions open to him.

Chapter 3 included the case of Debbie W., a young student who was inspired to become a counselor by the tragic experience of living with an alcoholic father. A highly motivated, capable, caring person, Debbie entered a two-year associate's degree program in drug and alcohol counseling at her local community college in the expectation that this degree would enable her to find employment and begin helping alcoholics and their families just as she had been helped. In her introductory counseling course her teacher took her aside and told her that to achieve her goals she would need more skills and more marketable credentials than an associate's degree would provide. Personal experience and empathic identification were not enough. He advised her to transfer to a four-year undergraduate program leading to a B.A. in psychology and then to consider taking a master's degree. He also made clear that no degree would give her all the preparation she needed. She needed work experience too—as much varied experience as she could get through volunteer work and internships. In the meantime, she would gain by having a few more years to explore her academic potential and develop her personal life instead of taking an immediate, emotionally charged plunge into counseling.

Debbie gratefully accepted this advice and transferred into the four-year program. The counseling she received exemplifies the constructive intervention that can sometimes save a trainee from subsequent disillusionment. By getting the benefit of such intervention while still in the stage of enthusiasm, Debbie could start her career on a realistic path instead of having to change course after suffering the effects of Burn-out. She was fortunate to learn this lesson much earlier than Roger F. did, but what she learned was essentially the same message that Roger got from the Medical Director. Which is not surprising, since the teacher who set Debbie straight was Roger himself.

The educational imperative is the same in other fields as in drug and alcohol counseling. Whether the degree in question is in psychology, social work, law, or nursing, additional schooling can open up options and point the way out of a rut. There is considerable ambivalence among people in the helping fields, though, about what else it does. Many people express doubts about whether what they learn in advanced-degree programs really helps them work with people. Obviously, the practical usefulness of academic training varies from field to field and from person to person. But perhaps the most important lesson to be learned from any course of instruction is that there is always more to learn.

What school unquestionably does provide is a change of scene. Where the focus is not on degrees and career advancement, but on the stimulation to be gained from the experience, going to school becomes an off-the-job intervention in the same sense as playing tennis or attending concerts. A young schoolteacher, imagining the grim prospect of having the same job ten years later, says, "To survive, I'd spend as little time as possible at my job. I'd get away, take a lot of courses—do anything to avoid burning out as a person." By "taking courses" she does not mean advancing herself professionally, but simply having another outlet in her life. Even before Roger F. ever had the idea of earning a degree, the satisfaction he got from taking college courses made it less devastating for him when one of his addict clients turned up in jail.

Making Adjustments on the Job

There are many ways to make a job more bearable. These include moving out of a live-in facility, switching from the night shift to the day shift, arranging for more on-the-job training and supervision, building "breathers" and "catch-up time" into a draining work schedule, clarifying responsibilities so as to apportion paper work and other drudgery more equitably, and instituting a team approach to dealing with clients. The possibilities are endless. Where they differ from the "legitimated malingering" we spoke of earlier is in their being fully legitimate, i.e., negotiated between the staff member and the institution in an above-board way so that there is no implication that the staff member is getting a special "break" or carrying less than a full work load. For example, a young psychiatrist brightens up an otherwise depressing job in a state mental hospital by contracting for weekly supervision by an eminent psychoanalyst. He is able to convince the hospital administration that this supervision will improve his performance sufficiently to justify the hospital's paying the analyst. Were he not successful in making this argument, he would have to make a value judgment about whether to pay the analyst himself.

Changing one's job description requires taking responsibility; it often requires considerable self-assertion. One who is getting work "dumped" on one's back by other staff members will have to speak up to put a stop to it, and even then one may not succeed. Some administrators are more open to reconsidering established patterns than others, and some organizational budgets allow for more flexibility than others. But it's worth a try.

An intervention that is becoming increasingly popular is

time sharing, whereby two people split the working hours and the remuneration normally assigned to one employee. One may work in the morning and the other in the afternoon, or they may work alternate days. Here the individuals involved are making a value judgment that they want to do part-time work for part-time pay. The institution gets the same services at the same cost as usual. There may be issues to be worked out regarding bookkeeping and fringe benefits, and the institution may suffer a loss in continuity of services to clients. There also is the question of how much ongoing practice in clinical procedures a person needs to remain effective. (Is too little work as bad as too much?) But the idea in principle is a sound one and has worked well where staff members have wanted it enough to make it work.

Changing Jobs

The case of Lynn M. showed that changing jobs sometimes works and sometimes does not. It's partly a matter of attitude and partly a matter of luck. There *are* jobs where the responsibilities, rewards, and results are more clearly laid out; where there is more direct contact with clients; where there is more (or less) individual responsibility; where there is more therapy and less custodial care; where women have more power; where there is less "politics" and bureaucratic maneuvering. The trick is to find them, which can be difficult when one knows what one is looking for and almost impossible when one does not.

Aside from finding a better job, there can be some value in changing jobs merely to gain exposure to new problems and new procedures. There is something to be said for varied experience both in building up an overall competence in the field and in rekindling enthusiasm (except when the job changes are used as an escape from meaningful commitment to any job). The person who is least likely to burn out is the one who is always finding new interests and new fields to conquer.

It is useful for staff members and personnel managers alike to evaluate how long a person continues to learn in a particular job and when stagnation sets in. For example, one year as an intake counselor in a social services agency may be long enough. But let us not forget the caveat from Chapter 9—that the job that might represent one's best opportunity may not be available out there in the real world, and that one may have to stay at one's present job longer than one's own needs and wishes might dictate.

Private Practice

One type of job change that is open to those with professional degrees is to go into private practice. Private practice has its problems too (isolation, uncertain income, unremitting work load), but it has one very alluring feature—the opportunity to "be your own boss." In private practice one has more chance than anywhere else to alter at least some of the "givens" in accordance with one's own values. But one has to be willing to pay the price, as Robert L. did.

Robert was a physician who took his medical degree and his family practice residency at major universities. With his reputation established at a leading medical school and its associated hospitals, he was assured of a successful career. But Robert was not satisfied with hospital-based medicine. Although determined to maintain the scientific standards in which he had been trained, he wanted to practice medicine with a personal touch. He wanted front-line contact with patients. He had, after all, become a physician so that he could be of service to families. At the same time, he would not willingly sacrifice the power and recognition that his university and hospital connections gave him. "How to enjoy both virtue and prestige" was his dilemma.

Together with a like-minded colleague, Robert attempted to set up first a family practice residency program, then a multispecialty group practice under the aegis of the university. The university and the various hospital departments paid lip service, as they naturally would, to the idea of giving families

24-hour physician service, home visits, continuity of care with a primary physician, and other such manifestations of medical "virtue." Nobody would be "against" those programs. But in reality no action was taken. As Robert later recalled, "We had to accept the fact that grown people could hold up their hands in an affirmative vote in a meeting and then do nothing to implement their decision." Institutional support was withheld because the interdisciplinary thrust of family practice threatened the bureaucratic fiefdoms of the established specialties.

Robert and his partner concluded that "we had to take care of ourselves. In our experience the people at major universities who were effective and fulfilled were those who had their own power base, usually in the form of a foundation or government grant." Since grants were not available to the two young physicians because of insufficient support from the university, they decided to establish their program as a private practice with a teaching program that would enable them to retain a nominal connection with the university.

To set up the practice they had to accept a number of sacrifices, which they saw as being justified by "our investment in ourselves and our autonomy." They had to take on entrepreneurial responsibilities. They had to go into debt. They had to operate in a highly competitive medical market where there was no guarantee that the unfamiliar concept of a community-based family practice would win over patients from established hospital-based specialists. For the first few years they had to draw subsistence salaries while alternating nights and weekends on call. In each case they were very clear about the value judgments involved. "I couldn't accept such an unbalanced life permanently," said Robert, "but for three years I consider it to be like starting any other business. I also probably couldn't maintain such a schedule if I were just teaching, administering, and doing research. It's the 'real' patient contact that keeps me going."

Within two years the practice was successfully launched. Robert and his partner still could not afford to hire a third physician to reduce their on-call hours, but they were seeing increasing numbers of patients who welcomed the services that were unavailable elsewhere. They were making house calls, delivering babies, counseling families, and seeing the entire spectrum of medical disorders. In addition, through the referrals they made as well as through teaching and hospital work, they remained actively in contact with their specialist colleagues. In their view, they had the best of both worlds. Furthermore, they had their own base of support—namely, their patients, as well as other appreciative constituencies such as medical students and local feminist groups. "Lack of appreciation by clients" was not a problem here:

> People tell us in the most vivid ways that what we're doing is valuable. They share their inner selves, take responsibility for their side of the relationship, and acknowledge and accept our capacity to make mistakes. Just the way they meet our gaze is nourishing.

In retrospect, Robert attributes their success to a willingness to take responsibility. "Nobody gave us this opportunity. We couldn't take anything for granted. The small amount of money we did get from the university could easily have gone elsewhere. We had to put every piece of this in place or else it wouldn't have happened." These two family doctors strikingly illustrate the way energy and a clear sense of value can produce a uniquely satisfying intervention. It should not be overlooked, though, that they began with the enormous advantages accorded by the M.D. degree. Furthermore, they showed extraordinary ambition, tenacity, enthusiastic dedication to their work, and a willingness to sacrifice a good part of their personal lives. (Robert and his wife separated while he was busy laying the groundwork for the practice.) Not everyone could, or would want to, do what they did.

But others are doing it in their own ways. What Robert L. is doing in medicine, Everett Z. is doing in law. One of "the new breed of family-oriented lawyers" that Lynn M. referred to, Everett has learned to do marriage counseling and family therapy as part of his law practice. Forsaking the usual adversary approach which, he says, "gives lawyers an incentive to divide people," he works with couples who want to reach amicable settlements. With all the divorce cases he has handled, he has been to court only twice in two years.

Like Warren C., the correctional counselor who gave up a supervisory position to go back to working with inmates, and Robert L., the modern-day family doctor who does not want to be "promoted beyond my competence" to a medical bureaucrat, Everett has been sufficiently aware of the costs of career advancement to turn down a judgeship. He, too, has made a value judgment in favor of working with people. For a while he was concerned about the financial sacrifice this course entailed. Then he came up with an ingenious intervention:

> I informally checked into the finances of a couple of lawyers who seemed to be doing much better than I was. With one, his father had money. With the other, his father-in-law had money. After that I stopped worrying.

Although willing to forgo the usual routes to career advancement, Everett is, in his words, always "extending my boundaries." He consults with human services professionals in order to learn new techniques for helping families work together. It is not coincidental that this man, who thoroughly enjoys his work, thinks it inconceivable that he will be doing exactly the same things in ten years.

Leaving the Field

At the opposite extreme from these highly fulfilled individuals are those who give up trying to help others as a vocation. Leaving the field can be a final despairing gesture or a considered judgment that one's skills and inclinations are not suited to the helping professions. It is not necessarily a defeat; for some people it is a good decision that leads to greater satisfaction and accomplishment in other fields.

Many individuals leave the human services for the private business sector, where, in the words of one ex-helper, "it isn't such a struggle to get people to respond." A psychiatric nurse announced her intention to give up nursing and get involved in business or the arts so that she could "see first-hand the broader world that clients live in and thus have a better perspective if and when I return to psychiatry." She is one of a growing number of women who are leaving traditionally "female" human services jobs in favor of the business positions now being made available to women by affirmative action programs. For years women were channeled into teaching, nursing, and social work without regard to aptitude or disposition. The desire to get out from under these stereotypes and master a new set of skills has taken many women into M.B.A. programs. Some are looking for the excitement that they observed (or thought they observed) in their fathers', husbands', or ex-husbands' business careers. They, like men, will find their share of problems and complications in this new field. But they will benefit from having a wider range of options, and the human services will benefit from having women and men come into the field because they choose to do so rather than because they have no other choice.

Off-the-Job Interventions: From Small World to Large

In the books that have followed *Reality Therapy,* such as *The Identity Society*[3] and *Positive Addiction,*[4] William Glasser contrasts the "failure identity" with the "success identity," "negative addiction" with "positive addiction," a survival-oriented, pain-escaping way of life with a disciplined, loving, fulfilled way of life. A person who moves from the one extreme to the other is moving from a "small world" to a "large world."

We have seen one small world in the stage of enthusiasm, where a person frequently is addicted to the job, and we have seen that world turn sour in the stage of stagnation. There the small world becomes a bar or staff lounge where disillusioned enthusiasts commiserate with one another.

Each person needs to make a value judgment about whether a small, job-centered world is enough. For a few achievement-oriented professionals it is. Robert L., the family physician, understands that "at some level I chose a type of medical practice where I'd always be answering the bell because I wanted it to be that way." He has accepted the consequences, including a broken marriage. Most people, however, are not perpetually inspired by their work, and for most people a balanced life is the most important intervention against Burn-out that there can be.

People who successfully avoid severe Burn-out problems almost invariably cite a degree of detachment from the job as contributing to their emotional balance. They say things like "I don't take on the identity of the program," or "The job isn't my whole being." To avoid total identification with one activity, though, they have to have an identity somewhere else. It is one thing to say that one is best able to do a good day's work when one can go home and forget about the job until the next day. But to be able to avoid taking work home one has to have someone or something to go home to.

Off-the-job interventions ultimately take precedence over on-the-job interventions. When one has made what adjustments are possible in the job situation, one still has to accept the job for what it is. One becomes able to do that when one's needs are being fulfilled elsewhere in life. Psychologists and sociologists talk about "networks" or "systems" in a person's life. Work is a system. Family life is a system. Social life, schooling, and recreation are all systems. In a healthy, satisfied person (leaving aside a few geniuses and other very dedicated individuals) the various systems exist in some kind of balanced relationship to one another. In each stage of Burn-out we have seen how difficulties in the area of work can adversely affect other systems, as when overwork damages one's health or strains a marriage. In the stage of intervention the idea is to reverse the process. When one strengthens other systems in one's life, one gains strength for coping with work as well.

The things people do to strengthen their "outside lives" and create a larger world to live in vary from individual to individual. Commonly mentioned off-the-job interventions include hobbies, travel, cultural activities, reading, exercise, participation in organized sports, family outings, and simply "getting away from it all." An important first step is to make a clear separation between work and other areas of one's life by limiting off-hours socializing with co-workers (or others in the same field) and controlling the tendency toward extracurricular preoccupation with on-the-job issues. One cannot usually control the number of hours one is required to work, but one can control what one does when one is not working. One can, for example, refuse to give friends and relatives free professional assistance with their personal problems. Where there is a question of giving out one's home phone number to clients so that one can be available to them in an emergency, one might consider whether the benefits for them outweigh the costs for oneself.

Probably the most important way of enlarging one's world is through close personal and family relationships. Developing and maintaining these relationships requires, and in turn creates, time commitments and emotional commitments that keep one from being swallowed up by the job. It may take a lot of work to negotiate with family and close friends the space one needs for one's commitment to the job and the space all concerned need to be together and to be away from constant reminders of the job. But it is by making this effort that one creates an identity independent of the job. There are, of course, many other reasons for wanting to be fulfilled in one's personal life. With regard to Burn-out, however, the importance of close personal ties is clear and crucial. When one is loved and appreciated by the folks back home, it is no longer a life-or-death matter whether one is loved and appreciated by clients or supervisors. When one enjoys the deep and constant support of family and friends, one is not putting one's whole self on the line when one goes off to work in the morning.

ORGANIZATIONAL INTERVENTIONS

Having emphasized the individual's primary responsibility to cope with Burn-out, we can return to the question of adjusting the work environment so as to reduce the severity of Burn-out and encourage positive involvement in staff members. A successful example of organizational change has occurred in the field of alcohol and drug addiction counseling in the 1970s, as described in Chapter 9. A key feature of this change has been the realization that staffing rehabilitation clinics with "quasi-patients" who are addicts one day and counselors the next is not good for either the counselors or clients. When newly recovering addicts are given a job for which they have not been sufficiently trained, their recovery as well as their ability to fulfill their duties is compromised. Realizing this, rehabilitation program administrators are now putting more emphasis on training. Recovering addicts, like everyone else, are employed as counselors when they can do the work of a counselor and command respect as such.

Although this is a special case, the lesson it points to is clear. Where Burn-out is plainly recognized as a problem, something will be done about it sooner or later. As recognition of the costs of Burn-out spreads from the frontline counseling milieu in areas such as addiction to the entire spectrum of human services, it can be expected that many human service organizations will attempt (as business and industry have been doing right along) to increase productivity and reduce discontent by providing a more supportive climate for staff members.

Some possible organizational remedies for Burn-out are

proposed by the distinguished organizational psychologist Robert Kahn.[5] One of these is to reduce the amount of time (per day, per year, and per career lifetime) that the helper spends working directly with clients. This could be accomplished in part by having people rotate between direct services and less stressful administrative and educational functions (an approach also recommended by Maslach). Kahn's notion of "career phases," by which a helper would phase out of direct services after a number of years in the way a basketball player moves up into coaching, is an interesting one, although for those who want to continue working directly with people it might only underscore the dilemma of having to give up direct client contact for the sake of career mobility. But for someone like Roger F., the drug counselor who left the front lines for teaching and consulting, the career phases Kahn envisions are highly relevant. Kahn also speaks of providing social support, on and off the job, for those employed in stressful situations (something that is easier said than done), whereas Maslach advocates peer support groups to give workers an outlet for ventilating frustration (which, as we have seen, can be a part of the problem as well as a solution).

Many of the issues that we have discussed—e.g., triage, staff polarization, legitimated malingering, time sharing, career development, community relations—are of particular concern to administrators. This list, however, could without much strain be extended to include practically everything discussed in this book. Administrators need to know what Burn-out is and how it happens; that is, how staff members feel about their jobs, what factors in the work environment lead to a loss of motivation and efficiency.

All the issues faced in the various stages of Burn-out can be translated into organizational interventions. These fall into two categories. One, representing the ideal, is to do something about the problem. Administrators certainly will want to respond to workers' concerns, alleviate problems, and improve working conditions where possible. There is an extensive literature about participatory management, training in actual job skills (including the often-overlooked skill of management), and other such measures. The testimony of administrators throughout this book, however, introduces a note of caution. There are limits to what administrators can do. Administrators are as constrained by the "givens" (budgets, bureaucratic politics, and so forth) as front-line workers. When it is not possible to change things, the only realistic intervention is to train staff members to cope with the existing conditions.

Reality Therapy, as applied to staff development, has two major tenets:

1. *Prepare staff members for what they can expect.*   Let them know what Burn-out is and what can and cannot be done about it. Show them how to recognize and deal with common problems contributing to Burn-out. Teach them to interpret individual failures as well as successes in the broader perspectives of the agency's overall program and the helper's career. Begin intervention as early as possible in training so that personnel can experience the process consciously rather than as a series of emotional reflex reactions.

2. *Do not interfere with natural consequences.*   Give support to staff members who are responsibly seeking to make constructive changes. But do not set up a small, artificial world where the rules of the real world do not apply. Do not create dependency by pampering employees, as with "legitimated malingering" or "quasi-patient" counselors. The clinic director who told drug counselors, "You're all replaceable!" was complimenting them. He was telling them that they were real people doing a real job.

An administrator, too, has to make a value judgment: Is your organization the kind where staff members go to a bar after work every day and talk about the supervisor (or, if the supervisor is with them, then the department head; or, if the department head is with them, then the chief administrator; or, if the chief administrator is with them, then the board of directors. . . .)? If it is, is that the kind of organization you want to have? Or do you want the kind of organization where there is leadership, discipline, modeling, goal setting, and an atmosphere of constructive guidance from the peer group as well as from management? If so, then putting into practice the principles we have outlined can be a step toward creating such an organizational climate—subject, of course, to the "givens."

INTERVENTION BY STAGES

As a quick review of the four stages of Burn-out, we can turn each stage on its head so as to indicate the aim of intervention in that stage:

1. *Enthusiasm–Realism.*   This is the best time for intervention—before the damage is done.
2. *Stagnation–Movement.*   Here is where further education and other interventions designed to get a stalled career going again are especially useful.
3. *Frustration–Satisfaction.*   In this stage the energy of discontent creates the possibility of change.
4. *Apathy–Involvement.*   If a person cares enough to be disappointed, is there a way to turn that feeling around?

Amid the distractions of organizational politics and the disillusionments of "the system," there is still the original purpose of helping people. Robert L., the hard-headed but still idealistic family physician, cuts through layers of hierarchical obfuscation with this view of his and other vocations:

> Nurses, orderlies, technicians complain about the menial tasks
> they have to do. These jobs have their menial side, but so does
> a doctor's. If you base your satisfaction on the task, where are
> you after your 3000th gastrectomy? That's not where the satis-
> faction is. It's by focusing on the human contact that you lift any
> job out of the menial category.

Effective interventions are those that remind the burned-out helper of the ideals and emotions evoked by the idea of working with people. A person who believes that it is still possible to help (within whatever constraints are operating) can remain active in the human services field. Without that faith there is little reason to stay in the field.

The inevitable experience of Burn-out can be, professionally speaking, a terminal experience or a growth experience. Thinking of frustration or depression as an educational experience may not make it more pleasant, but understanding its place in the rhythm of our development can help us be at peace with it.

"In all birth there is pain," said a person struggling back from disillusionment. There is pleasure as well, and the meaning of our life and work comes from accepting the pain and pleasure that are natural consequences of our actions.

NOTES

CHAPTER 2

1. Stanton, A. H., & Schwartz, M. S. *The mental hospital.* New York: Basic Books, 1954.

2. Freudenberger, H. J. Staff burn-out. *Journal of Social Issues,* 1974, *30* (1), 159–165; The staff burn-out syndrome in alternative institutions. *Psychotherapy: Theory, Research and Practice,* 1975, *12*(1), 73–82. (Reprinted by the Drug Abuse Council, Washington, D.C., 1975.)

3. Hendrickson, B. Teacher burnout: how to recognize it; what to do about it. *Learning,* January 1979, 37–39.

4. Ellison, K. W., & Genz, J. L. The police officer as burned-out samaritan. *FBI Law Enforcement Bulletin,* March 1978, 1–7. Maslach, C., & Jackson, S. E. Burned-out cops and their families. *Psychology Today,* May 1979, 59–62.

5. Maslach, C., & Jackson, S. E. Lawyer burnout. *Barrister,* Spring 1978, 8, 52–54.

6. Shubin, S. Burnout: The professional hazard you face in nursing. *Nursing 78,* July 1978, 22–27.

7. Pines, A., & Maslach, C. Characteristics of staff burnout in mental health settings. *Hospital and Community Psychiatry,* 1978, *29,* 233–237.

8. Maslach, C., & Pines, A. The burn-out syndrome in the day care setting. *Child Care Quarterly,* 1977, *6,* 100–113.

9. Hall, R. C. W., Gardner, E. R., Perl, M., Stickney, S. K., & Pfefferbaum, B. The professional burnout syndrome. *Psychiatric Opinion,* April 1979, 12–17.

10. Duffy, J. C., & Litin, E. M. *The emotional health of physicians.* Springfield, Ill.: Charles C Thomas, 1967. Fox, J. D. Narcotic addiction among physicians. *Journal of the Michigan State Medical Society,* 1957, *56,* 214–217. Modlin, H. C., & Montes, A. Narcotics addiction in physicians. *American Journal of Psychiatry,* 1964, *121,* 358–365. Small, I. F., Small, J. G., Assue, C. M., & Moore, D. F. The fate of the mentally ill physician. *American Journal of Psychiatry,* 1969, *125,* 1333–1342. Winick, C. Physician narcotic addicts. *Social Problems,* 1961, *9,* 174–186.

11. Maslach, C. Burned-out. *Human Behavior,* September 1976, 16–22; The client role in staff burn-out. *Journal of Social Issues,* 1978, *34*(4), 111–124; Job burnout: how people cope. *Public Welfare,* Spring 1978, 56–58.

12. Maslach, C., & Jackson, S. E. A scale measure to assess experienced burn-out: The Maslach Burn-Out Inventory. Paper presented at the meeting of the Western Psychological Association, San Francisco, April 1978.

13. Pines, A., & Kafry, D. Occupational tedium in the social services. *Social Work,* 1978, *23,* 499–507, p. 500.

14. *Ibid.,* p. 504.

15. Maslach, The client role in staff burn-out, p. 121.

16. Argyris, C. *The applicability of organizational sociology.* Cambridge, England: Cambridge University Press, 1972. Katz, D., & Kahn, R. L. *The social psychology of organizations.* New York: Wiley, 1966. Likert, R. *The human organization.* New York: McGraw-Hill, 1967. Litwin, G. H., & Stringer, R. A. *Motivation and organizational climate.* Boston: Division of Research, Harvard Graduate School of Business Administration, 1968. Tannenbaum, A. A. *The social psychology of the work organization.* Belmont, Cal.: Wadsworth, 1966. Vroom, V. H., & Deci, E. L. *Management and motivation.* Penguin, 1976.

17. Kahn, R. Job burnout: prevention and remedies. *Public Welfare,* Spring 1978, 61–63.

18. Carkhuff, R. R. *Helping and human relations: A primer for lay and professional helpers.* Vol. 1, *Selection and training.* New York: Holt, Rinehart and Winston, Inc., 1969. Carkhuff, R. R., & Berenson, B. G. *Beyond counseling and therapy.* New York: Holt, Rinehart and Win-

ston, Inc., 1967. Truax, C. B., & Carkhuff, R. R. *Toward effective counseling and psychotherapy: Training and practice.* Chicago: Aldine Publishing Company, 1967. Wolf, S. An investigation of counseling type, client type, level of facilitative conditions and client outcome. (Doctoral dissertation. Washington, D.C.: The Catholic University of America, 1970.) *Dissertation Abstracts International,* Ann Arbor, Mich.: University Microfilms, No. 70-22,093.

19. Wolf, S. Counseling—for better or worse. *Alcohol Health and Research World,* Winter 1974/75, 27–29.

CHAPTER 3

1. Silverstein, L. M. *Consider the alternative.* Minneapolis: CompCare Publications, 1977.

CHAPTER 4

1. Asch, S. E. Studies of independence and conformity: A minority of one against a unanimous majority. *Psychological Monographs,* 1956, *70*(9).

2. Glasser, W. *Positive Addiction.* New York: Harper and Row, 1976.

CHAPTER 5

1. Silverstein, L. M. *op. cit.*

2. Sheehy, G. *Passages: Predictable crises of adult life.* New York: Dutton, 1976.

CHAPTER 7

1. Frank, J. D. *Persuasion and healing.* Baltimore: Johns Hopkins University Press, 1961.

2. Wolf, S. Counseling—for better or worse. *Alcohol Health and Research World,* Winter 1974/75, 27–29.

CHAPTER 10

1. See articles cited in Chapter 2.

2. Kopp, S. B. *If you meet the buddha on the road, kill him.* Palo Alto, Cal.: Science and Behavior Books, 1972.

3. Peele, S. *Life-sized therapy: Putting the therapy experience in perspective.* New York: New American Library, in press.

4. Glasser, W. *Reality therapy.* New York: Harper Colophon Books, 1975, p. 30.

5. For a comprehensive analysis of the dynamics of addiction as an experience (whether or not the addiction is to a drug) see Peele, S. (with Brodsky, A.) *Love and addiction.* New York: New American Library, 1976.

6. Sidney Simon's work in "values clarification" can be very helpful in learning to make clearer, more decisive value judgments. See Simon, S. B., Howe, L., & Kirschenbaum, H. *Values clarification.* New York: Hart, 1972.

7. Ellis, A., & Harper, R. A. *A new guide to rational living.* N. Hollywood, Cal.: Wilshire, 1975.

8. Horney, K. *Neurosis and human growth.* New York: Norton, 1950.

CHAPTER 11

1. Frank, J. D. *op. cit.*

2. Silverstein, L. M. *op. cit.,* pp. 81–82.

3. Glasser, W. *The identity society.* New York: Harper & Row, 1972.

4. Glasser, W. *Positive addiction.* New York: Harper & Row, 1976.

5. Kahn, R. *op. cit.*

BIBLIOGRAPHY

Ellis, A., & Harper, R. A. *A new guide to rational living.* N. Hollywood, Cal.: Wilshire, 1975.

Ellison, K. W., & Genz, J. L. The police officer as burned-out samaritan. *FBI Law Enforcement Bulletin,* March 1978, 1–7.

Frank, J. D. *Persuasion and healing.* Baltimore: Johns Hopkins University Press, 1961.

Freudenberger, H. J. Staff burn-out. *Journal of Social Issues,* 1974, *30*(1), 159–165.

Freudenberger, H. J. The staff burn-out syndrome in alternative institutions. *Psychotherapy: Theory, Research and Practice,* 1975, *12*(1), 73–82. (Reprinted by the Drug Abuse Council, Washington, D.C., 1975.)

Glasser, W. *Mental health or mental illness.* New York: Perennial Library, 1970.

Glasser, W. *The identity society.* New York: Harper & Row, 1972.

Glasser, W. *Reality therapy.* New York: Harper Colophon Books, 1975.

Glasser, W. *Positive addiction.* New York: Harper & Row, 1976.

Hall, R. C. W., Gardner, E. R., Perl, M., Stickney, S. K., & Pfefferbaum, B. The professional burnout syndrome. *Psychiatric Opinion,* April 1979, 12–17.

Hendrickson, B. Teacher burnout: how to recognize it; what to do about it. *Learning,* January 1979, 37–39.

Kahn, R. Job burnout: prevention and remedies. Public Welfare, Spring 1978, 61–63.

Maslach, C. Burned-out. *Human Behavior,* September 1976, 16–22.

Maslach, C. The client role in staff burn-out. *Journal of Social Issues,* 1978, *34*(4), 111–124.

Maslach, C. Job burnout: how people cope. *Public Welfare,* Spring 1978, 56–58.

Maslach, C., & Jackson, S. E. Lawyer burnout. *Barrister,* Spring 1978, 8, 52–54.

Maslach, C., & Jackson, S. E. A scale measure to assess experienced burnout: The Maslach Burn-Out Inventory. Paper presented at the meeting of the Western Psychological Association, San Francisco, April 1978.

Maslach, C., & Jackson, S. E. Burned-out cops and their families. *Psychology Today,* May 1979, 59–62.

Maslach, C., & Pines, A. The burn-out syndrome in the day care setting. *Child Care Quarterly,* 1977, *6,* 100–113.

Peele, S. with Brodsky, A. *Love and addiction.* New York: New American Library, 1976.

Pines, A., & Kafry, D. Occupational tedium in the social services. *Social Work,* 1978, *23,* 499–507.

Pines, A., & Maslach, C. Characteristics of staff burnout in mental health settings. *Hospital and Community Psychiatry,* 1978, *29,* 233–237.

Shubin, S. Burnout: The professional hazard you face in nursing. *Nursing 78,* July 1978, 22–27.

Silverstein, L. M. *Consider the alternative.* Minneapolis: CompCare Publications, 1977.

Simon, S. B., Howe, L., & Kirschenbaum, H. *Values clarification.* New York: Hart, 1972.

Wolf, S. Counseling—for better or worse. *Alcohol Health and Research World,* Winter 1974/75, 27–29.

INDEX

3 5282 00608 3706